Teaching Tactical Creativity in Sport

Creativity is an essential component of sport performance. The player who can make decisions that are both unexpected – and therefore less easily predicted by his/her opponent – and appropriate is the player who is likely to be successful. In this ground-breaking new book Daniel Memmert explores the concept of tactical creativity, introducing a new theoretical framework based on extensive empirical research. He argues for the importance of encouraging divergent thinking abilities at an early age, and explains how tactical creativity sits alongside conventional approaches to "teaching games for understanding". The book outlines essential rules for environmental and training conditions, and suggests a wide range of game forms for teaching and coaching tactical creativity to children and young people. This is important to all students, researchers, coaches and teachers working in physical education, sports coaching, sport psychology or skill acquisition.

Daniel Memmert is a Professor and Head of the Institute of Cognitive and Team/ Racket Sport Research at the German Sport University of Cologne with a visiting assistant professorship at the University of Vienna, Austria. He is a football and tennis coach with a PhD in cognition and a habilitation in creativity in team and racket sports from the Elite University of Heidelberg. His research interests are cognitive science, human movement science, computer science, and sport psychology. He has 15 years of teaching and coaching experience, and has published more than 120 peer-reviewed publications and 35 books or book chapters. Daniel is a reviewer for several international (sport) psychology journals and transfers his expertise to business companies and several professional football clubs (e.g. German Bundesliga, Champions/Europa League).

ROUTLEDGE STUDIES IN PHYSICAL EDUCATION AND YOUTH SPORT
Series Editor: David Kirk, University of Bedfordshire, UK

The *Routledge Studies in Physical Education and Youth Sport* series is a forum for the discussion of the latest and most important ideas and issues in physical education, sport, and active leisure for young people across school, club and recreational settings. The series presents the work of the best well-established and emerging scholars from around the world, offering a truly international perspective on policy and practice. It aims to enhance our understanding of key challenges, to inform academic debate, and to have a high impact on both policy and practice, and is thus an essential resource for all serious students of physical education and youth sport.

Also available in this series

Children, Obesity and Exercise
A practical approach to prevention, treatment and management of childhood and adolescent obesity
Edited by Andrew P. Hills, Neil A. King and Nuala M. Byrne

Disability and Youth Sport
Edited by Hayley Fitzgerald

Rethinking Gender and Youth Sport
Edited by Ian Wellard

Pedagogy and Human Movement
Richard Tinning

Positive Youth Development Through Sport
Edited by Nicholas Holt

Young People's Voices in PE and Youth Sport
Edited by Mary O'Sullivan and Ann Macphail

Physical Literacy
Throughout the lifecourse
Edited by Margaret Whitehead

Physical Education Futures
David Kirk

Teaching Tactical Creativity in Sport

Research and Practice

Daniel Memmert

Routledge
Taylor & Francis Group

LONDON AND NEW YORK

First published 2015
by Routledge
2 Park Square, Milton Park, Abingdon, Oxon OX14 4RN

and by Routledge
711 Third Avenue, New York, NY 10017

Routledge is an imprint of the Taylor & Francis Group, an informa business

British Library Cataloguing-in-Publication Data
A catalogue record for this book is available from the British Library

Library of Congress Cataloging in Publication Data
A catalog record has been requested for this book

ISBN: 978-0-415-74590-1 (hbk)
ISBN: 978-1-315-79761-8 (ebk)

Typeset in Times
by Saxon Graphics Ltd, Derby

MIX
Paper from
responsible sources
FSC
www.fsc.org   FSC® C013604

Printed and bound by CPI Group (UK) Ltd, Croydon, CR0 4YY

With love to Kerstin, Kim and Lina

Contents

Figures and tables

Figures

Tables

Preface

According to popular opinion, there is great potential in creative moments, products and processes. They can be the motor of success, progress and top performance in a variety of contexts such as economics, science and sports. Creative ideas can lead to adequate solutions, despite the presence of endless numbers of bad or vague problems without prefabricated approaches. Which possibilities – called "golden eggs" in Japanese companies – do businessmen, managers, working group leaders, teachers, coaches, sport managers and other executives need to encourage their employees, children and players to pursue in order to develop original solutions to a problem?

The present textbook proposes creative behaviour as a new aspect of teaching and research in the training and development of creativity or divergent thinking, using sports as the key example. Therefore, the purpose of the book is to analyse divergent thinking from the perspectives of cognitive psychology, human movement science, computer science and social psychology. The focus of the text will be on the detailed clarification of the psychological contribution of visual attention, motivation, the environment and domain-specific expertise for the development of divergent tactical performances in team and racket sports, how the development of tactical creativity can be displayed in training programmes, the basic conditions that are important in the development of creativity in team and racket sports, and how creativity can be measured in team and racket sports.

In a very general manner and without concrete definition, the first chapter introduces the term creativity in terms of everyday life, industry, politics, business and sports, and underlines the importance of creative ideas and thinking processes in our lives. The second chapter is dedicated to how psychology and computer science have conceptualised creative thinking in recent decades and which scientific theories have been derived. In addition, the chapter reviews recent literature in the area of general school education and creativity. Creativity in physical education and team sports is then described in Chapter 3, and a definition of the term "tactical creativity" is introduced. This chapter also demonstrates that tactical creativity must be developed early in life, and that the term creativity is a component that is missing in current models of teaching team and racket sports. Therefore, a new paradigm for teaching tactical creativity in team and racket sports – the so called "Tactical Creativity Approach" (TCA) is presented in

Chapter 4. Here, the text will discuss the dynamical system approach, an implicit learning approach, tactical transfer investigations and the importance of variability, which are all integrated in the tactical creativity approach in great depth.

Chapter 5 discusses the TCA more thoroughly as a theoretical framework for developing tactical creativity. Empirical evidence is presented that supports rules for environmental conditions and methodological aspects of the respective training units. Studies are described that attempt to provide evidence for direct and indirect environmental influences on the development of team and racket sport players who have the ability to make unconventional but adequate decisions in complex game situations (**Deliberate Play**). This chapter also completes the transition between theory and practice through the description of specific game forms to train tactical creativity (1-**D**imension Games). In addition, experimental field studies are outlined showing that the perception of many situations in different team and racket sports (football, handball, field hockey, tennis, table tennis) positively influences the development of divergent tactical cogitations (**D**iversification).

Furthermore, Chapter 5 discusses why attentional mechanisms could potentially be responsible for the development of creative behavioural patterns (for a review, see Memmert, 2009b). This branch of research, based on fundamentals, highlights the connection between visual attention processes and cognitive performance (e.g. tactics, creativity). At the outset there is a theoretical substantiation of why the inattentional blindness paradigm (Most, Scholl, Clifford and Simons, 2005; Simons and Chabris, 1999) promises insight with regard to creative behaviours. This includes empirical evidence that inattentional blindness is not correlated with other components of attention. In addition, connections between inattentional blindness, expertise and divergent performances become apparent in general, as well as in sport- and game-specific settings.

Building on the aforementioned studies, experiments on cognitive-tactical decision making show that the focus of attention can be influenced by very simple variations in instructions, and that these variations directly affect the quality of tactical performances (**Deliberate Coaching**). These studies confirm that the reported insights could be implemented in new types of training programmes in such a way that creativity in team ball sports can be fostered. Training programmes with fewer instructions to the players lead to a greater amount of unusual tactical responses.

Finally, current research will be reviewed highlighting the possibilities and opportunities available to physical education to consider motivationally-oriented theories in the accomplishment of sport performances and tactical creativity (**Deliberate Motivation**). Additionally, current results are presented that show that the Regulatory Focus Theory developed by Higgins (1997) affects the creativity-moderating variable attention and can foster tactical creativity. Moreover, further studies indicate that it is the manner and length of training (**Deliberate Practice**) during youth that has influenced the creativity of current league and national team players.

The sixth chapter describes three methods that show how tactical creativity can be measured in team sport: game observation, game test situations, and creativity tests. Here, new findings in computer science provide possibilities for evaluating creative solutions rapidly and accurately. Chapter 7 will present examples of teaching units demonstrating how teachers and coaches can foster tactical creativity in different kinds of basic tactical game forms.

The textbook ends with theoretical and sport practical implications in Chapter 8. With TCA as a theoretical platform, it is possible to create a wide range of game forms for teaching and coaching tactical creativity in physical education classes and training sessions. Considered together, the findings discussed in this book highlight the fact that TCA can play a useful role in promoting the development of tactical creativity in children. Therefore, the purpose of this textbook is to offer new aspects for teaching and fostering tactical creativity in team and racket sports. The TCA creativity model suggests that keeping conditions playful encourages greater learning effects for children in team and racket sport games.

This textbook demonstrates that it could be possible and especially rewarding for businessmen, managers, working group leaders, teachers, coaches, sport managers and other executives to examine the conditions that underlie creative ideas with a more scientific approach. Sport games are an ideal example for this, due to their complexity.

In addition, this book is written to help student teachers and coaches teach creativity in team and racket sports. The issues and principles could be important for different kinds of sports such as football, ice hockey, team handball, basketball, field hockey, softball, volleyball, beach volleyball, tennis, table tennis, American football, rugby, badminton, cricket, baseball or squash.

As an example, this textbook is targeted to students studying Physical Education, Sports Coaching or Applied Sports Pedagogy in graduate classes. For undergraduate courses this could be an optional text given to students while trying to introduce an innovative approach to teaching games. At the graduate level this textbook could be a core text providing a solid basis on how tactical creativity is fostered in team and racket sports. Therefore, after a short summary discussion at the end of each chapter, questions are raised to prompt students to think about the issues in the chapter and reflect on the content in other situations. In addition, further important and extended literature is mentioned to provide students and teachers with more detailed information and sometimes the original source of the content given in the chapter.

I would like to thank many friends and colleagues with whom I was able to do research and publish the studies reviewed in this book during past years, and who have provided valuable direct or indirect encouragement for this book: Joe Baker, Rouven Cañal-Bruland, Philip Furley, Pablo Greco, Andreas Grunz, Robert Hristovski, Stefanie Hüttermann, Stefan König, Henning Plessner, Jürgen Perl, Klaus Roth, Bernd Strauß, Daniel Simons and Christian Unkelbach. Of course, this also includes all the students and participants who provided essential contributions to the experiments in this book. Additionally, I also want to thank the members of our Institute of Cognitive and Team/Racket Sport Research at the German Sport University in Cologne, Germany, and others for the proofreading and editing of this book, namely Frowin Fasold, Philip Furley, Stefanie

Hüttermann, Stefan König, Carina Kreitz, Fabian Liesner, Alex Moraru, Ben Noel, Karsten Schul, and Bente Wegner, as well as Cornelia Reese for creating the Figures. I am especially thankful to Fabian Liesner for his extensive contribution to the editing process. A "creative" research programme rarely results from the idea of an individual person, but rather from the common thoughts of many in a comfortable atmosphere. Finally, I hope you will enjoy reading the book, as it contains essential knowledge about how to foster creativity in team and racket sports.

1 Creativity

An introduction

Creativity in real life

The terms uniqueness, originality, intuition or creativity have assumed a meaningful and individual position in our society during the last sixty years. Creative accomplishments often reveal bizarre ideas or the unusual behaviour of people, and seem to not involve analytical and rational thoughts. Accordingly, creativity is connected to imagined or hidden processes, and thus it appears to deny scientific access. A current example of this is one of the best football players in the world, Lionel Messi (Figure 1.1). Fabio Cannavaro, a former Italian world class footballer and now a coach, said of him: "In the way he plays, Messi gives the audience the illusion that the spontaneous and wild on the street still exists. How can you stop him? Shut your eyes and pray!" Or: "Messi is the most incredible player I have ever seen," says basketball phenomenon Kobe Bryant. And: "The truth is that it amazes me when the best player in the world continues inventing things that I have never seen before. Messi is a very creative player and you never know what he is going to do with the ball. He creates excitement for the fans every time he touches the ball."

Examples of creative products can be found in all eras: the infantile composition by Wolfgang Amadeus Mozart, the invention of the light bulb by Thomas Edison, the chemical structure of the benzene ring, or the discovery of the Fosbury Flop in the high jump (see Figure 1.2). In addition, a well-known joke refers to a creative solution of a problem. Out of the blue, two men are facing a seemingly hungry lion in the desert. While one of them runs away in panic, the other one calmly puts on his running shoes. While running, the fleeing man shouts: "You don't really think that you'll be faster than the lion with those shoes, do you?" "No," the guy says composedly, "but I'll probably be faster than you."

In team and racket sports, rehearsed action sequences (e.g. moves) often lead to creative success. However, creative tactical ideas play an important role in many cases. For example, in football, the midfield players have the task of controlling the team's developing game by clever tactical decision-making behaviour. Similarly, "playmakers" in handball or basketball can set up finishing options for their team mates with creative solutions.

Figure 1.1 Lionel Messi (FIFA World Player of the Year in 2010, 2011 and 2012) with the author of this book at the training centre of FC Barcelona in May 2011

Figure 1.2 Creativity in sport: a new high jump technique (© Original by Helmut Wegmann, pixelio.de; www.pixelio.de)

Examples of creative players based on statements from football experts:

"Messi plays on a completely different level." (Neymar)

"Next to Ribéry we have one more who can bring creativity better into the game on a narrow space. We want to improve ourselves. This can only work with extraordinary players." (Van Gaal, about Robben)

"He makes the difference, he brings unpredictability into the game and carries the team with him." (Beckenbauer, about Robben)

"At his appearance, you can see how much fun he has playing football. He is an incredibly creative person." (Reus, about Götze)

"With his tricks, Özil dominates the art of the unexpected!" (The Spanish newspaper El Pais)

These examples could be continued endlessly. In our everyday lives and working environments we are confronted with new situations for which we do not have learned and prepared solutions. Nevertheless, we manage to look for answers which let us cope with the tasks. All these examples demonstrate that creative solutions are central facets of life, concerning business life, professional life, and sports. Managers must find new ways to solve problems for industrial productions; designers must develop creative solutions in industrial or web design to secure crucial competitive advantages; and football players must make decisions in specific sporting situations which are unexpected and therefore less predictable for their opponents. Most of these original solutions are context-specific, embodied in emotions, and have a motivational background (Memmert, Hüttermann and Orliczek, 2013). So how do people find more creative solutions?

Creativity research has been approached in a multitude of domains as diverse as science itself – for instance, literature, music, art, religion, and politics (for an overview see Milgram, 1990; Runco, 2007; Sternberg, 1999; Sternberg and Lubart, 1999). First and foremost, in a general and scientific context, Sternberg and Lubart (1999, p. 3) define creativity as "the ability to produce work that is both novel (i.e., original, unexpected) and appropriate (i.e., useful)" (for more detail, see Chapter 3). Therefore, the term "creativity" stands in contrast to the term intelligence (cf. also Chapter 3). Intelligence was the key variable for the description of intellectual skills according to the classic intelligence models of Thurstone (1938), Guilford (1956) or Cattell (1971), which have subsequently experienced modifications and extensions. Gardner (1993) names seven types of talents in his "multiple intelligences" model: linguistic, logical-mathematic, visual-spatially, musical, physical-kinesthetic, intrapersonal and interpersonal intelligence.

While intelligence is always connected with the only right (convergent) solutions, the term creativity stands for productive, original, shaping, artistic, artful, inventive, innovative, imaginative, enterprising, fanciful, groundbreaking or trend-setting solutions, to name just a few descriptors. Generally speaking, creative behaviour means creating ideas leading to adequate solutions of a tricky problem without prefabricated approaches. These solutions are often recognised as surprising, original and flexible within their environment. The central aim of this textbook is to discuss creative thinking in complex situations such as team and racket sports in order to analyse creative performance and its development in real world environments, as recommended by many investigators (Lieberman, 2000; Runco and Sakamoto, 1999; Simonton, 2003).

Creativity in industry, politics and business

To the greatest possible extent, nowadays there is agreement in economics, industry and politics that inventiveness and creativity have developed to become the central factors for the success of an enterprise. As an example: Robert Sternberg, the world's leading scientist in creativity research, reports the garbage men in New York who had to face the time-consuming problem of picking up big and heavy dustbins from backyards, and then putting them back after emptying them before returning to the garbage truck. After a while, the men realised that it would be much more economical and faster (saving one trip) if they didn't return the empty dustbins to their original place, but instead – because they are all the same size and colour – brought them to the next backyard where they picked up the next full dustbin. This saved almost 50% of the costs and working hours.

> "Creativity is one of the key factors of an innovative society. The development of creative capital needs creative people, as well as an appropriate environment that makes living and working at certain places more attractive." (Hans-Heinrich Grosse-Brockhoff, Cultural State Secretary in North Rhine-Westphalia, September 18th 2007). In September 2007 Jürgen Rüttgers (the Premier of North Rhine-Westphalia) announced the investment of a total of 50 million euro for transfer strategies until 2012, in order to increase the number of patents and to encourage technology-orientated foundations.
>
> The German Chancellor Angela Merkel said: "Germany is once again able to demonstrate their long-standing power as a country of fruitful ideas. Frequently there were innovative ideas by German thinkers changing the world. Our two Nobel Prize winners are well-known examples of that. In the future, let us be the country of ideas that makes action out of ideas, and action will provide chances for everybody. These were, are and will be the strengths of Germany."

For 75% out of 1070 managers from industry, the topic of innovation is one of the top three priorities of their business strategies, and for 40% of them it is the primary priority (worldwide survey of the business consultancy Boston Consulting Group). As Hasso Plattner (SAP founder and chairman of the board) suggests: "For a long time people spoke only about how to economise costs. Now many companies recognise that if it is not possible to keep profit they are not at all able to grow. One can only grow if one is seriously innovative."

The concerns of creativity in the field of economics are also supported by numerous statistics (Jansen, 2006; Florida, 2002). In the European Union almost 6.5 million people, and 25% to 30% of the working population in developed industrial countries, work in the sector of creativity – for instance, in advertising, design, music, film, fashion or media – which is even more than in the chemical or car industries. In the USA these creative industries are believed to generate even more income than the industrial and service sectors put together. In 2004 the "creative class" (Florida, 2002) generated 2.6% of the gross domestic product of Germany, which is comparable with the chemical and car industry. The peak year turnovers are made by the sectors of culture (82.0 billion euro), software/computing (18.4 billion euro) and advertising (11.8 billion euro).

The importance of creativity in the economic field, and the large number of optimistic results has led to a rethinking and a reorientation of companies, managers, work-group leaders and other managers. Professor Robert Sternberg recently made the following statement to the German press about the importance of creativity in politics and economics: "Have a look at the current situation in the financial sector. We are going through a global crisis, only caused by misplaced credits of the banks. Only the investment bank Goldmann and Sachs has succeeded in escaping the danger. They have not only recovered their losses; they even made profits – although they had exactly the same information as their competitors. Creative, flexible thinking is not a luxury – it is a necessity."

Today, terms like "autonomy" and "self-monitoring at work", with a focus on long-term, self-initiated experiences, are becoming increasingly popular. This popularity is an argument for the establishment of creativity-supporting environments in companies and workplaces where employees are mostly independent, which would make non-compliant and unconventional work possible. Thus, management is more facilitating than directing. Bennis, Heil, and Stephens (2000) associated the optimal behaviour of managers with the behaviour of parents or teachers, which is focused more on growth and development than on productivity.

Based on Ekvall and Ryhammer (1999), an atmosphere that supports creativity can be established in companies by six factors: (1) make the achievement of employees' goals possible, so their work is relevant; (2) give appropriate opportunities for such achievement; (3) support employees' ideas, (4) instill confidence; (5) make regular, free exchange of ideas possible; and (6) permit or even support adventurous behaviour.

A range of questionnaires has been constructed which allows companies and organisations to assess the potential of their own atmosphere and environment for innovation. For instance, Kasof (1997) found that as a result of loud noise people focus their attention on solving a task even more than usual. Therefore, the width of their focus of attention necessarily decreases. As a result, they are less successful in creating original solutions than other experimental subjects, who solved the same creative tasks without auditory interruptions and who were therefore able to handle the tasks with a wider focus of attention without isolating themselves from their environments.

Overall, a form of communication in companies that includes employees seems to play an important role. Werth, Denzler and Förster (2002) showed that rewards, which are focused on profit and non-profit, lead to improved performance in creative tasks, but at the same time decrease analytical thinking.

The assessment of Germany as a location by Professor Herbert A. Henzler (business consultancy McKinsey), published in the magazine "sports" in December 1998, states the following: "In the 70s and at the beginning of the 80s, German football was world-leading. In the field of sport we were at the very forefront, and coaches from all over the world came to Germany to receive training. However, in the past few years we did not keep pace particularly in technique and tactics – almost similar to the society and the economy. One can find connections between a lack of innovation in economics and in sport. At the beginning of this century German technicians, entrepreneurs and scientists created a flourishing industrial society by a wave of inventions and new manufacturing processes. Today other countries are leading in innovations. To make Germany successful again, thinking barriers have to be overcome and routinised training methods have to be abandoned. Only those who have the nerve to experiment can succeed in the future."

The science of economics takes a similar view: "Creativity is a basic element of human life, a widely laid out social process, which requires cooperation. This is stimulated by human exchange and networks; it takes place in actual communities and in real places" (Florida, 2002, p.23). Thus, competition for the most attractive locations and workplaces for creative people has already begun. This is underlined by the formation of megalopolises (metropolitan areas which are created by the merging of several cities), like the ones developing in Tokyo or "Boswash" (the metropolitan area between Boston and Washington). Megalopolises will be "creative oases", the success centres of the global economy of the twenty-first century.

Summary

In this first chapter I have taken a first wide view of the meaning of creativity in everyday life, but also in industry, business and politics. Without a doubt, it has become clear that creative ideas are becoming more and more meaningful in all areas. Hand in hand with this goes the belief that human progress can only be successful when innovative ideas and developments help to create new possibilities for human beings. Not only time can be saved, for example, but also things can be achieved and performances accomplished that were not possible before these creative solutions.

Discussion questions

1 What is the difference between intelligence and creativity?
2 Name products or ideas in our society that you consider to be creative.
3 Try to think of historical events and creative inventions in history that dramatically and sustainably changed society.
4 Which measures could firms and commercial enterprises take to support the creativity of their employees?

Additional reading

Florida, R. & Tinagli, I. (2004) *Europe in the Creative Age.* London: Demos Publications.
Guilford, J.P. (1967) *The Nature of Human Intelligence.* New York: McGraw Hill.
Kasof, J. (1997) Creativity and breadth of attention. *Creativity Research Journal*, 10, 303–315.
Sternberg, R.J. (ed.) (1999) *Handbook of Creativity.* Cambridge: Cambridge University Press.

2 Creativity in science

Creativity in psychology

The analysis of creative thinking is a very popular contemporary topic among psychologists (for an overview, see DeDreu et al., 2012). Prominent examples are the American creativity researchers Roberta Milgram, Mark Runco and Robert Sternberg, who have published the essence of their research in a variety of books. In the last decade, creativity research has regained popularity (Csikszentmihalyi, 1999; Damasio, 2001), mostly due to extraordinary findings in the field of modern functional neuroanatomy (Cabeza and Nyberg, 2000; Dietrich, 2004).

Findings from neuroscience regarding the relation between creativity and alpha brain wave activity have indicated an overall condition of strongly pronounced internal perception in the cortex during creative thinking processes (Fink and Benedek, in press). Several studies have shown a slight increase in alpha activity in the posterior parietal areas of the right hemisphere, which could demonstrate the important combination or re-combination of conceptually distinct and unrelated semantic information for creative thinking (e.g. Fink et al., 2009; Fink, Graif and Neubauer, 2009). The posterior cortex is supported by the frontal lobe, which is involved in a number of higher cognitive processes; this region plays an important role in intelligence, working memory and deductive thinking. Moreover, important planning, control and supervisory functions of thinking processes are attributed to the frontal lobe. Creative thinking contains a range of cognitive processes that are attributed to the frontal brain: cognitive flexibility, focus or defocus of attention, the (new) combination of stored thought content, or the evaluation of the feasibility and practicability of an idea (cf. Heilmann et al., 2003). The increase of alpha activity in the frontal cortex that was observed in a number of creativity studies (for a review Dietrich, 2004) could represent a state in which the frontal brain regions, in a top-down manner, are not influenced by distracting, task-inconsequential cognitive processes (cf. Sauseng et al., 2005; von Stein & Sarnthein, 2000), so that a smooth production of creative ideas could be guaranteed.

Modern neuroscience-based studies have found evidence that analytical, intelligent thinking happens in the left hemisphere of the brain whereas creative thinking is assigned to the right hemisphere (see Figure 2.1). Of course, for many

Left and Right Brain Functions

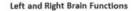

Left-Brain Functions		Right-Brain Functions
Analytic thought		Holistic thought
Logic		Intuition
Language		Creativity
Science and math		Art and music

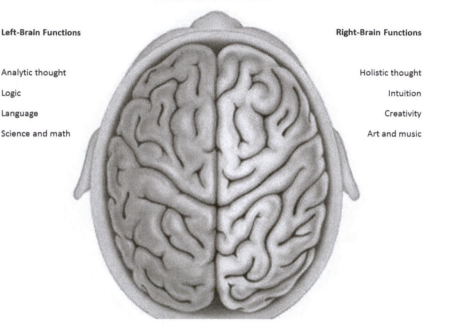

Figure 2.1 Classification of different cognitive abilities into both brain functions (from www.learn.ppdictionary.com/)

tasks we need both hemispheres and thus both ways of thought processing: when we face a problem, we try to find possible solutions (divergent thinking) before we choose one of the options (convergent thinking). Hence, the two hemispheres are subject to a high degree of interaction.

Creativity models have a very interesting history (for more details see Runco, 2007) but for this textbook, the focus will be on the work of Robert J. Sternberg. According to his integrative model known as the "Investment Approach to Creativity: Buy low, sell high" (Sternberg and Lubart, 1991, 1992, 1995), he managed to incorporate different theoretical designs in one framework (cf. Figure 2.2). This framework includes the Componential Theory of Amabile (1983), the Systems Approach developed by Csikszentmihalyi (1988), the Synectic Model of Gordon (1961) and the Triarchic Theory of Intelligence developed by Sternberg himself (1985). Furthermore, it includes results from studies on personality (Barron, 1965), problem solving (Getzels and Csikszentmihalyi, 1976), creative styles (Kirton, 1976), and different environmental influences (Simonton, 1988).

As shown in Figure 2.2, the authors distinguish four different levels in their model, namely interacting resources (1), domain-specific "creative" abilities (2), a portfolio of "creative" projects (3), and assessments of "creative" products (4). Originally, the model aimed to illustrate the creative process from the start (the required resources and abilities) to the end (the assessment of the product).

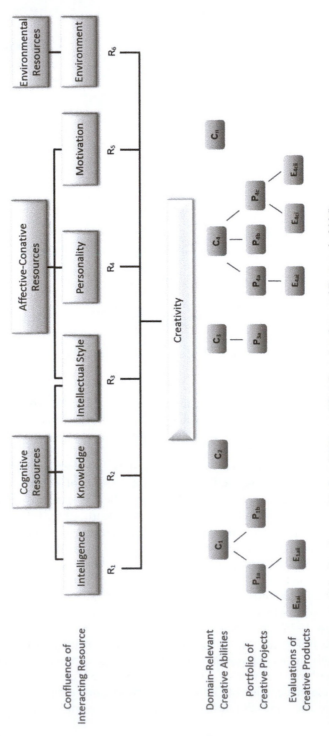

Figure 2.2 Creativity model by Sternberg and Lubart (1991; modified from Amelang and Bartussek, 2006)

"Because creativity is moderately domain-specific, it needs to be measured in specific domains, and through meaningful domain-related activities" (Sternberg and Lubart, 1992, p. 5).

According to Sternberg and Lubart (1991), there is an array of six resources (R_{1-6}; see Figure 2.2): intelligence, knowledge, intellectual style, personality, motivation, and environment. Sternberg and Lubart (1991, p. 5) further assume that all resources are subject to a complex interrelation, and that they are interdependent with regard to the generation of domain-specific, creative solutions (level 2; C_{1-n}) in a given task. In a first multivariate validation study ($N = 48$), the authors showed that five of the resources – the environment factor was not taken into consideration – gave an exact prediction of creative performance (measured as the sum of scores from subjects' drawings, stories, scientific problem solving and so on) with a multiple correlation coefficient of $R = .81$. The evaluation of the cognitive and affective-conative resources was conducted by means of an extensive test battery (cf. in more detail Sternberg and Lubart, 1991), with fluctuations in the inter-correlations of the predictor variables between .09 and .68 (Mdn = .32).

In Chapter 4, based on the theoretical framework of Sternberg and Lubart (1991), a sport-specific creativity model will be introduced with a focus on the improvement of creative performances in team and racket sports. Special attention will be given to the following resources: intelligence (e.g. attention processes), environment, and motivation. In addition, this creativity model will illustrate the component model by Sternberg and Lubart (1991), which provides the theoretical framework for the individual studies we conducted (presented in Chapter 5 and 6).

Creativity in computer science

Nowadays, the statement that creativity is a stochastic, combinational process (Dietrich, 2004; Martindale, 1999; Simonton, 2003) is broadly accepted. This means that creative thinking is characterised by unsystematic drifting, that it is chaotic and thus allows for the emergence of loosely connected associations (cf. Chapter 4, see dynamical systems theory). Martindale (1995) used a wide variety of examples (e.g. associative hierarchies, defocused attention) to demonstrate that major theories of creativity can be transferred into computer science approaches and modeled with connectionist theories, as both are nearly identical. For these reasons, computer science and computational psychology seem to be suitable for modelling ill-defined, creative performance without any a priori detailed predications or explanations (e.g. Boden, 2003). Overall, net-supported (qualitative) processes seem to be a worthwhile starting point for inter- and intra-individual analyses of creative performances. This is due to the fact that embedding them in multidimensional assessment frameworks can provide valuable additional information about these processes.

Memmert and Perl (2009a) showed that a neural networks approach is a suitable means to analyse and simulate creative behaviour. First, learning processes were separated individually by the "Dynamically Controlled Networks" Approach (DyCoN; Perl, 2004a). As a result, specific characteristics and distinctive features

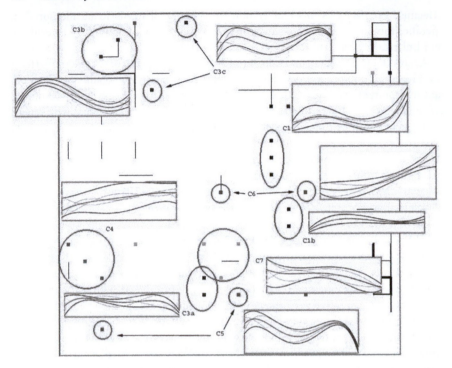

Figure 2.3 Trained network with marked clusters of neurons representing typical profiles: the profiles are mathematically smoothed from sets of corresponding original time series and embedded in the respective maximum and minimum profiles (Memmert and Perl, 2009b)

of learning processes can be better understood, such as, for instance, fluctuation behaviour (see Figure 2.3). The results demonstrated that with regard to the development of creativity, five types of learning behaviour can be distinguished (cf. Memmert and Perl, 2009a). Only two of them display a consistent profile with constant or even improved performance. A third type shows a continuous deterioration, and the two remaining types – down-up as well as up-down fluctuation processes – show strange behaviour with alternately increasing and decreasing performance. In both cases, the creative performance increases initially, but at the end, as can be seen from the yellow square step, the performance is worse than in the middle of the training session and vice versa.

These results are useful for the further development of existing theories from computer science. For example, the results reveal that the development of divergent thinking could be accounted for by the Performance Potential Meta Model (PerPot, cf. Perl, 2004b), which was originally developed in order to analyse physiological adaptation processes. The use of Performance Potential Meta Model here is based on the assumption that creative behaviour can also be understood as a dynamic adaptation process (e.g. Boden, 2003; Simonton, 2003). Typical results of Performance Potential Meta Model analyses are two delay values: delay in strain and delay in response. These values characterise the extent to which an organism's performance is adapted to the training load stimulus. The Performance Potential Meta Model demonstrated that these fluctuations in learning appear systematically as transient effects in antagonistic adaptation processes and are shaped by specific factors that characterise the lags in re-learning and re-forgetting. The five empirical types of learning behaviour correspond well with PerPot's simulated theoretical profiles. If the delay in strain is smaller than the delay in response, strain becomes effective first, causing decreased performance (up-down fluctuation process), which is later compensated by the delayed response (super-compensation effect). If the delay in response is smaller than the delay in strain, the response becomes effective first (down-up fluctuation process), causing an initial improvement, which can later be stabilised or reduced depending on the delayed impact of strain. Such adaptive dynamics called for further attempts to analyse learning behaviour with neuronal networks in two ways: through process patterns and through simulation of learning behaviour as dynamic processes as a whole (cf. Chapter 4).

While further information was generated from convergent thinking (Memmert and Perl, 2005) and divergent tactical performance values (Memmert and Perl, 2006; Memmert and Perl, 2009b) by means of conventional neuronal network assessment (Kohonen Feature Maps), Memmert and Perl (2009b) developed a novel approach with the extension of "seldom events" to simulate creative behaviour (see Figure 2.4). Therefore, the concept of DyCoN (Dynamically Controlled Networks) had to be extended to "natural" learning. One important point was dynamically adapting the capacity of the network to the requirements of the learning process. This was achieved by integrating the concept of Growing Neural Gas (GNG; see Fritzke, 1997) in which – briefly explained – the number and positions of neurons vary time-dependently with the changing information flow from training, adapting the network topology to the amount and content of the training. The result is the Dynamically Controlled Neural Gas (DyCoNG), a combination of the DyCoN and the GNG, which is a network that completes neurons that represents the quality of information and can therefore measure the creativity of any recorded activity (cf. Figure 2.5 a, b and c).

Technically speaking, the areas of acceptance of each neuron in a DyCoNG are restrained by an individually varying sphere. Therefore, the so-called Voronoi cells cover the entire input area of the network, resulting in the mapping of each input stimulus to its corresponding, most-similar neuron. Consequently, rare input stimuli (e.g. those associated with creative activities) are aggregated to a most-similar frequent type of input.

The DyCoNG-approach (Memmert and Perl, 2009a) was established using data from a longitudinal field-based study with nine measurement times. The creative behaviour in standardised test situations was analysed in a creative training programme that lasted for half a year. The results from DyCoNG-based simulations have demonstrated that this network is able to differentiate between qualitative and quantitative clusters, generate connections between clusters, and separate main types of divergent thinking processes. In addition, the network is able to reproduce recorded, creative learning processes by means of simulation. The qualitative analogies between real and simulated creative learning processes correspond surprisingly well.

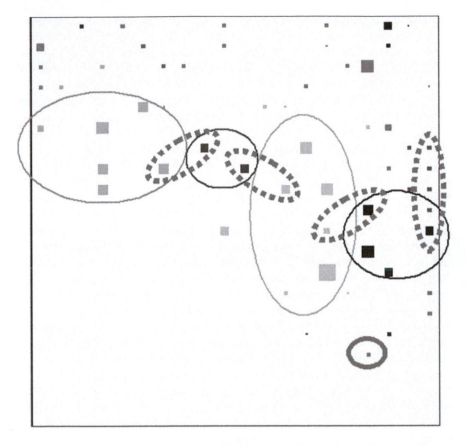

Figure 2.4 Net with clusters (marked by thin lines), associative "jumps" between clusters (bold dotted lines), and generated quality neuron (bold line; Memmert & Perl, 2009b)

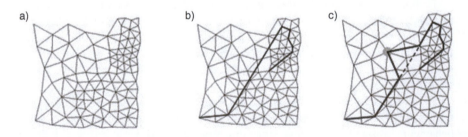

Figure 2.5 a) 2-dimensional projection of a Growing Neural Gas with areas of high density (top right), low density (left), and medium density, b) 2-dimensional projection of a Growing Neural Gas with a process trajectory; c) Example of a trajectory containing a creative neuron (grey circle), representing a rare and adequate action (cf. Perl, Memmert, Bischof and Gerharz, 2006)

Creativity in education

Meta-analyses of the effectiveness of different training programmes to improve creativity currently exist (Scott, Leritz and Mumford, 2004). Based on seventy studies, research demonstrates that well-designed creativity intervention can indeed foster divergent thinking in a number of different domains. More successful training programmes focus more heavily on cognitive skills using realistic settings in the investigated domain. However, when looking for more educational programmes in schools that attempt to foster general divergent thinking, one can find only few publications (e.g. Garaigordobli and Berruseco, 2011; Haddon and Lytton, 1968; Olive, 1972; Tuckman and Hinkle, 1986). Tuckman and Hinkle (1986) compared the physical and psychological effects of running to those of a regular physical education lesson in a study with younger school children. The results showed that running improved children's cardiorespiratory health as well as their general creativity. Garaigordobli and Berruseco (2011) evaluated the effects of a play programme on the creative thinking abilities of preschool children. They found that the programme increased not only their verbal creativity (fluency, flexibility, originality) and their graphic creativity (elaboration, fluency, originality) but also their behaviour and traits of the children's creative personalities. Likewise, Chapman (1978) and Haddon and Lytton (1968) investigated playfulness and the development of divergent thinking abilities in primary school children with similar results. It seems that playfulness and stimulus seeking displayed at a young age may correlate with a particular way of thinking in later years. Additionally, Olive (1972) showed a similar relationship between divergent thinking and intelligence, social class, and achievement in a study with high-school students.

In summary, three points will be highlighted here: first, the studies discussed above give an understanding of the importance of implementing creative programmes for preschool children. Second, in recent studies education and teaching have been at the centre of the investigation, not physical education and sports. Third, in this kind of research, general assessments and evaluations of divergent thinking were used, as opposed to sport-specific measurements to indicate divergent tactical thinking (cf. Chapter 7).

Summary

In Chapter 2 I have introduced different kinds of concepts and empirical findings from the fields of psychology, computer science and education. First, the theoretical framework of Sternberg and Lubart (1991) was discussed as a general approach for understanding the nature of creativity. Six resources were suggested to be important in creativity: intelligence, knowledge (expertise), personality, motivation, intellectual style, and environment. According to Sternberg and Lubart (1991), all these resources are interdependent with regard to the production of domain-specific creativity, and they could be interpreted as a complex interconnection in a given situation. In addition, we have seen that modern computer scientists can model creativity with neuronal networks. For example, Memmert and Perl (2009b) developed a novel neuronal network approach to simulate rare events. Here, rare input stimuli (e.g. creative solutions) are aggregated to a most-similar frequent type of input. Last but not least, education studies give us a better understanding of the importance of implementing creative concepts in schools. However, these recent findings were conducted in neither physical education nor in sports. In addition, sport-specific tests of divergent thinking skills are missing completely.

Discussion questions

1   Explain the creativity theory of Sternberg and Lubart (1991).
2   Why are basic approaches from computer science, such as neuronal networks, qualified to analyse and simulate creative behaviour?
3   Which central results were achieved by neuronal networks and what conclusions can be drawn for further research in sports with regard to practical implications?
4   Which possibilities do teachers have to support their students' general creative behaviour?

Additional reading

Csikszentmihalyi, M. (1999) Creativity. In R.A. Wilson & F.C. Keil (eds.), *The MIT Encyclopedia of the Cognitive Sciences* (pp. 205–206). Cambridge: MIT Press.

Damasio, A.R. (2001) Some notes on brain, imagination and creativity. In K. H. Pfenninger & V. R. Shubik (eds.), *The Origins of Creativity* (pp. 59–68). Oxford: Oxford University Press.

Martindale, C. (1999) The biological basis of creativity. In R. J. Sternberg (ed.), *Handbook of Creativity* (pp. 137–152). Cambridge: Cambridge University Press.

Memmert, D. & Perl, J. (2009a). Game Creativity Analysis by Means of Neural Networks. Journal of Sport Science, 27, 139–149.

Memmert, D. & Perl, J. (2009b). Analysis and Simulation of Creativity Learning by Means of Artificial Neural Networks. Human Movement Science, 28, 263–282.

Milgram, R.M. (1990) Creativity: An idea whose time has come and gone. In M. A. Runco & R. S. Albert (eds.), *Theory of Creativity* (pp. 215–233). Newbury Park: Sage.

Runco, M.A. (2007) *Creativity – Theories and Themes: Research, Development, and Practice*. Burlington: Elsevier Academic Press.

Ward, T.B., Finke, R.A. & Smith, S.M. (2002) *Creativity and the Mind – Discovering the Genius Within*. Cambridge: Perseus Publishing.

3 Creativity in physical education and team and racket sports

For more than thirty years, models have been developed in different countries on how to introduce team and racket sports in schools or clubs. The Teaching Games for Understanding approach (Bunker and Thorpe, 1982), the Tactical Games Approach (Mitchell, Oslin and Griffin, 2006), Play Practice (Launder, 2001), Game Sense (Den Duyn, 1997; Light, 2004), the Tactical Games Model (Metzler, 2000), the Invasion Games Competence Model (Tallir, Lenior, Valcke and Musch, 2007), the Games Concept Approach (Rossi, Fry, McNeill and Tan, 2007) and finally the Tactical-Decision Learning Model (Grehaigne, Wallian and Godbout, 2005) are well-established approaches for teaching and coaching, offering children and students ways of learning both tactical and technical skills in different games. These approaches initially focus on the teaching and development of an understanding of the tactical dimensions of game play (i.e. what to do), before the teacher/instructor focuses on the development of the students' technical skills associated with the game (i.e. how to do it) (cf. Grehaigne, Godbout and Bouthier, 1999). Thus, the primary aim of these teaching and coaching approaches is to teach tactical problem solving in different types of invasion games (e.g. basketball, netball, football etc.).

Currently, the initial Teaching Games for Understanding model developed by Bunker and Thorpe (1982) is gaining importance as the latest findings in situated learning (Dodds, Griffin and Placek, 2010) and non-linear learning processes (Chow, Davids, Button, Shuttleworth, Renshaw and Araújo, 2007) lead to a re-thinking of the model (cf. in detail, Kirk and MacPhail, 2009). "In particular, we suggest that explicit attention to the learner's perspective, game concept, thinking strategically, cue recognition, technique selection, and skill development as the clustering of strategies and techniques, and situated performance as legitimate peripheral participation in games, elaborate upon the already existing but implied learning principles of the Bunker-Thorpe model" (Kirk and MacPhail, 2009, pp. 280–281).

Based on a literature review, Oslin and Mitchell (2006) recommended more contextual and ecological research regarding game-centred approaches. Another review on game-centred approaches was published recently. In this review Harvey and Jarrett (2013) argued that a number of significant challenges remain for game-centreed approaches. For example, more manipulation checks, improved assessment tools, longitudinal research designs, and longer intervention programmes are needed.

In conclusion, two points define game-centred approaches; first, they are models that place the learner into problem solving situations, where decision-making is of critical importance and where skill development takes place in context. Second, these approaches focus on the teaching of game sense, game playing ability, or even game performance. This means that tactical intelligence is being trained and developed. Thus, children have to learn convergent tactical thinking (see Chapter 1). Our approach will focus on the development of tactical creativity, and will be explained in more depth in the next chapter.

Definition of creativity

For teaching and coaching team and racket sports, the above approaches advocate the need for contextual, real-world and game-simulated practice to develop both the tactical and technical skills needed to become an effective game player (e.g. Holt, Strean and Bengoechea, 2002; Mitchell, Griffin and Oslin, 1995; Turner and Martinek, 1992). In this chapter, a competency property will be presented and discussed that has not yet been an intentional component of the previously mentioned approaches for teaching and coaching: tactical creativity.

The distinction between expert decision making (e.g. tactical intelligence, game sense) and creativity may be based on the theoretical distinction between "divergent thinking" and "convergent thinking" (Guilford, 1967; see also Chapter 2). Convergent thinking refers to the ability to find the ideal solution to a given problem. Therefore, a clear and structured task with an obvious objective can be performed with a best solution strategy that can later be evaluated as the optimal result by the environment. In team and racket sports this is similar to tactical decision making, game playing ability or simple game sense. In contrast, Sternberg and Lubart (1999, p. 3) define divergent thinking as the unusualness, innovativeness, statistical rareness or uniqueness of solutions in a given task on a behavioural level. In team and racket sports this is reflected in tactical creativity which produces varying, rare and flexible decisions in different situations (Memmert and Roth, 2007; Roth, 2005). Michael Jordan, Magic Johnson, Ricky Rubio and Steve Nash are well-known examples of basketball players who use highly unusual and original passes. Even when intending to pass the ball to player A, they are able to perceive if player B is suddenly unmarked and better positioned at the last second and pass the ball to the other available player instead. Thus for team and racket sports, two cognitive thinking processes can also be differentiated: tactical game-intelligence and tactical creativity.

In summary, in the domain of team and racket sports, deviating from the so-called best solutions (convergent tactical thinking, game sense, game playing ability), creativity (divergent tactical thinking) is understood as the surprising, original and flexible production of tactical response patterns (Memmert and Roth, 2007; Roth, 2005).

Definition

- **Tactical intelligence (convergent tactical thinking):** In team and racket sports, tactical game intelligence is understood as the production of the best solution for specific individual, group or team tactics in match situations.
- **Tactical creativity (divergent tactical thinking):** In team and racket sports, tactical creativity is understood as the generation of a variety of solutions in specific individual, group and team tactics situations which are surprising, rare and/or original.

Tactical intelligence vs. tactical creativity

There are a variety of studies in the field of psychology that address the relationship between divergent and convergent thinking (see Runco and Albert, 1986; Yamamoto, 1965). For the explanation of variance between divergent and convergent thinking of about 20% to 30%, different models of correlation are discussed (see Cropley, 1995). Alongside the summation-, capacity- and canal-model, the threshold-model attracts the strongest interest (see Figure 3.1a,b). It is assumed that high intelligence is not correlated with creativity, however, high creativity requires an outstanding intelligence.

In a study by Memmert and Roth (2007), the tactical creativity and tactical intelligence of children with an average age of seven years was determined at three measurement points (T0 to T2; respectively intervals of six and nine months). For this study, divergent and convergent game test situations were developed by Memmert (2007; see Chapter 6 for more details). Performance on these tasks was rated by three educated and independent judges, and the ratings were averaged later. In a re-analysis, 213 children were available at T0 (Fig 3.2a), 223 at T1 (Fig 3.2b) and 176 at T2 (Fig 3.2c). To examine the threshold model, the intelligence

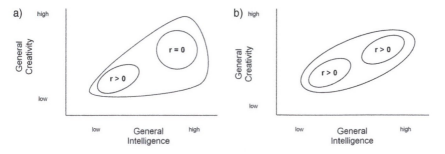

Figure 3.1 Connection between intelligence and creativity: a) this threshold-model reference shows that high convergent mental capacity is not mandatorily identical with high divergent mental capacity; b) this model assumes that a high convergent mental capacity normally correlates with high divergent mental capacity

continuum was divided into four sections following Runco and Albert (1986) as well as Ginsburg and Whittemore (1968). On the one hand, these sections were defined by similar sample sizes in the individual areas; on the other hand, the sections were defined by interval distances (cf. Figure 3.2). For both sub-samples the following analysis steps were chosen in the style of Runco and Albert (1986): the visual inspection of the scatter plots followed by the assessment of standard deviation, which is based on average values (constants) of faults containing the distances between y-points (creativity parameters) and a linear regression line [(Y-Y')2/n], as well as on correlation coefficients.

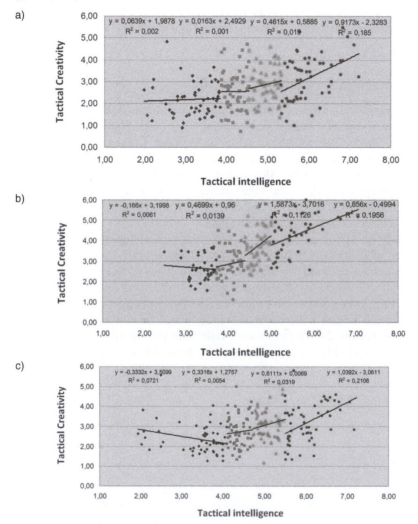

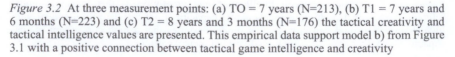

Figure 3.2 At three measurement points: (a) TO = 7 years (N=213), (b) T1 = 7 years and 6 months (N=223) and (c) T2 = 8 years and 3 months (N=176) the tactical creativity and tactical intelligence values are presented. This empirical data support model b) from Figure 3.1 with a positive connection between tactical game intelligence and creativity

The evaluation agreement between the convergent and divergent thinking performances can be rated as very good (95% of intra-class correlation coefficients >.80). Correlation coefficients between divergent and convergent performance indexes of .36, .55 and .71 were obtained for the three measurement times, respectively. These correlation coefficients are located in a similar area as in other psychological studies (cf. Yamamoto, 1965; Runco and Albert, 1986). The scatter plots at T0, T1 and T2 are presented in Figure 3.2 a to c, from top to bottom in four sections with linear regression lines.

The differences between the four areas in the number of data points, independent of the examination time, show that the available data cannot support a threshold model. As a general rule, small variances or greater correlation coefficients do not appear in the first sections and no high variances appear in the last sections. In ten of twelve situations, no significant differences appear between the single sections for the dependent variable standard deviations, faults or correlation coefficients. Only for the dependent variable standard deviations both first intervals differ from the last. In summary, if there is any relationship at all, a higher game intelligence seems to be accompanied by higher creativity. In future studies, age and sample related effects should also be considered.

Golden years of learning: "Sooner rather than later"

Many psychological studies have shown that creativity must be learned and developed early in life (for a review, see Milgram, 1990). Recent research from neuroscience suggests that stagnation in creativity development may occur after the age of eight (Huttenlocher, 1990). Children up to the age of seven years exhibit the greatest absolute number and density of synapses in the human primary visual cortex, as well as resting glucose uptake in the occipital cortex (see Figure 3.3). These indicators are associated with creativity (Ashby, Valentin and Turken, 2002). In recent years, we have conducted numerous studies of children dealing with the development of tactical creativity (for a review, see Memmert, 2011).

Primary results from a cross-sectional design by Memmert (2010b) support the evidence from neuroscience and also indicate that creativity should be cultivated early in a child's development. Comparisons between age constellations assume that children and adolescents (peer groups: seven, ten and thirteen years) do not appear to develop linearly in their creative performance (see Figure 3.4 a to d). In the range of seven to ten years, considerable increases in tactical creativity are important to highlight. This may be connected to the fact that the absolute number of synapses and the synapse density has reached its maximum at the years before. In summary, training sessions with children should focus on developing tactical creativity. By improving divergent tactical thinking abilities early in the training process, the teaching of team and racket sports and the measurement of its success can focus on tactical creative thinking that probably cannot be developed and improved in later training phases. After childhood, the sensitivity to training in creativity becomes weaker.

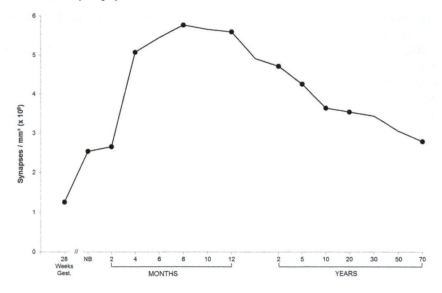

Figure 3.3 The development of synapse density in the human primary visual cortex (modified from Huttenlocher, 1990)

Using a longitudinal design, Memmert (2010a) analysed intra-individual improvements in the German Football Association's (Deutscher Fußball-Bund, DFB) young talents in football-specific tactical creativity. A total of 195 talents aged twelve and thirteen years participated in additional goal-oriented training in the DFB talent promotion programme once a week, while also maintaining their regular football club training. Across all four DFB bases, the general results showed that during the six-month observation period, on average no deterioration or improvement in tactical creativity appeared, as was evident through evaluation by game test situations (cf. Chapter 6). Nevertheless, there was a slight tendency for younger athletes to improve more. This indicates that above the age of thirteen years, the development of tactical creativity stagnates. However, a more specific examination of the data revealed that more than half of the talents improved their tactical creativity, even though the time period was only six months long. Twelve subjects improved their divergent thinking scores by more than 5%, and 20 by more than 10%. Three twelve-year-olds and two thirteen-year-olds even improved their creative performance by more than 20%. In contrast, the development of nine players declined by more than 20%. This suggests a large potential for intra-individual improvements in tactical divergent thinking tasks. Furthermore, the results point out that very different change processes could be observed in the players. Accordingly, some subjects reacted very positively to tactical creativity training impulses in training sessions at their clubs.

All in all, it can be concluded that coaches (or teachers) should integrate exercises that concentrate on the development of divergent tactical thinking abilities in their training units as early as possible. After childhood, the effect of training activities on tactical creativity seems to become weaker but is still evident.

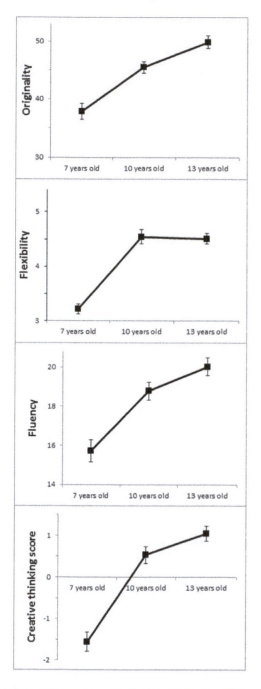

Figure 3.4 The development processes of tactical creativity for children and adolescents at the ages of seven, ten and thirteen years, differentiated by a) fluidity (first diagram in row), b) flexibility, c) originality and d) a total value of creative thinking. All three characteristic values of creativity were determined by video creativity tests (Memmert, 2010b)

Summary

By means of the Teaching Games for Understanding approach, the factors and importance of several game-centred approaches were discussed. In contrast to convergent tactical thinking or decision making which should be trained by game-centred approaches, tactical creativity as a kind of divergent thinking ability was introduced in more detail in this chapter. Tactical creativity is defined as the generation of surprising, seldom and original solutions in specific tactical situations in team and racket sports. Empirical data shows that there are some overlaps between tactical intelligence and tactical creativity, but both should be interpreted as different kinds of thinking skills. For the development of tactical creativity the golden years of learning start sooner rather than later. In addition, initial empirical evidence suggests that there is a strong improvement of tactical creativity until the age of ten years. Afterwards, the influence of training on creativity becomes increasingly weaker.

Discussion questions

1   Which well-established approaches for teaching and coaching exist, and what are their similarities and their differences?
2   What is the difference between tactical intelligence and tactical creativity in team and racket sports?
3   What are the connections between tactical intelligence and tactical creativity, and how can they be established by current theoretical models and empirical data?
4   Discuss the empirical evidence in favour of coaching and teaching tactical creativity in children as early as possible.

Additional reading

Grehaigne, J.F., Wallian, N. & Godbout, P. (2005) Tactical-decision learning model and students' practices. *Physical Education and Sport Pedagogy*, 10, 255–269.
Griffin, L.A., Mitchell, S.A. & Oslin, J.L. (1997) *Teaching Sport Concepts and Skills: A Tactical Games Approach*. Champaign: Human Kinetics.
Guilford, J.P. (1967) *The Nature of Human Intelligence*. New York: McGraw Hill.
Launder, A.G. (2001) *Play Practice: The games approach to teaching and coaching sports*. Champaign, IL: Human Kinetics.
Memmert, D. (2010a) Testing of tactical performance in youth elite soccer. *Journal of Sports Science and Medicine*, 9, 199–205.
Memmert, D. (2010b) Creativity, Expertise, and Attention: Exploring their Development and their Relationships. *Journal of Sport Science*, 29, 93–104.
Mitchell, S.A., Oslin, J.L. & Griffin, L.L. (2006) *Teaching sport concepts and skills: A tactical games approach* (2nd ed.). Champaign: Human Kinetics.
Runco, M.A. & Albert, R.S. (1986) The threshold theory regarding creativity and intelligence: An empirical test with gifted and nongifted children. *Creative Child and Adult Quarterly*, 11, 212–218.

4 Learning and teaching within the scope of the tactical creativity approach in team and racket sports

Through the development of versatile and sometimes extraordinary solutions, named *divergent* tactical thinking, a significant and domain-relevant ability for teaching and coaching in team and racket sports is recognised (see Chapters 2 and 3). Wayne Gretzky was known for his uncanny ability to see three moves ahead of the play at hand and hold the whole game in his mind. This insight, as Sidney Crosby, a twenty-three-year-old hockey player describes, is the ability to see "not where everyone is when you look, (but) where everyone will be if you buy some time and hold the puck for another second" (Allen, 2004, cited in Walinga, 2007). In team and racket sports, this particularly concerns the tactical creativity which is defined by varying, rare and flexible decisions in different kinds of situations.

Some of the basic issues in research on cognition and action in team and racket sports are related to problems in the nature and use of information by players. What is important for generating possible decisions and for seeking original solutions is that one player is able to perceive all the important information from his or her environment (the positions of team mates and opponents, players emerging unexpectedly etc.) and to factor this into an action plan. In some studies it has been proposed that environmental information is available to performers in advance. In many experiments information has usually been held constant over trials so that the athletes merely have to make a decision and respond accordingly. For example, in traditional cognitive science approaches to studying reaction times (e.g. Schmidt and Wrisberg, 2004), the main emphasis and the relation between the amount of unpredictability (e.g. information content) of environmental events and reaction time of the athletes is treated as a decision-making performance variable. This approach remains vague with respect to the following question: how is this information created in sport contexts? In other words, the amount of information studied in this experimental approach had to be introduced into the explanation in an *ad hoc* manner, and it was not a constituent that could be derived from within the explanatory models.

Next the dynamical system approach, the implicit learning approach, tactical transfer research, and the effects of variable learning conditions underpinning the TCA will be discussed in more depth. These factors all highlight aspects of teaching that are important for the development of tactical creativity.

The dynamical systems theory

The seminal experimental study by Kelso (1984) and the mathematical models that followed in the subsequent years (Haken, Kelso and Bunz, 1985; Schöner, Haken and Kelso, 1986) showed how it is possible for complex movement systems to manifest abrupt self-organisation under the change of some independent variables, such as movement frequency. These elementary, bimanual self-organisation effects were soon extended to more complex movement systems with more intricate and spontaneous self-organising effects, such as relative coordination (Jeka, Kelso and Kiemel, 1993) and learning effects (Zanone and Kelso, 1992). This research has produced a significant amount of knowledge on the self-organising capacities of neurobiological systems with oscillatory behaviour containing fewer degrees of freedom. In recent years, the emphasis has been on extending these ideas, among others, to problems of posture (Bardy, 2004; Bardy, Marin, Stoffregen and Bootsma, 1999), discrete movements (Jirsa and Kelso, 2005), and cognitive processes (Port and Van Gelder, 1998).

Recent investigations in human movement science (for a review see Davids, Button and Bennett, 2007; see also Araújo, Davids, Bennett, Button and Chapman, 2004; Handford, Davids, Bennett and Button, 1997; Williams, Davids and Williams, 1999) have shown how goal-oriented behaviour in team and racket sports, including decision making, can be explained by the concepts of spontaneous self-organisation under constraints in a range of different sports (Hristovski, Davids and Araújo, 2006; Araújo, Davids and Hristovski, 2006; Araújo et al., 2004, 2005; Passos et al., 2006).

The main characteristic of the Nonlinear Dynamical Systems Theory is that it emphasises the study of biological movement systems under the constraints of their natural environments, focusing on the parametric control of such systems (see Kelso, 1995). For example, perceptual information is a non-specific source of data that can be harnessed to regulate the directional or timing characteristics of a movement. It is non-specific because it does not specifically inform the dynamical characteristics of a movement system; for example, it does not contain kinetic or kinematic movement information.

Nonlinear Dynamical Systems Theory emphasises qualitative changes in the system rather than dealing merely with quantitative metrics (for a similar qualitative analysis example, see the neuronal network approach in Chapter 2). This theory is specifically interested in and suited for dealing with events that manifest abrupt changes as a result of a minor change (theoretically infinitely small) in the space of the independent variables (i.e. the control parameter space). According to the linear view, natural cognitive systems function so that there is a proportional relation between the independent causes and their effects. Nonlinear Dynamical Systems Theory deals with linear thinking (i.e. the linear approximation case) with a remarkably counterintuitive behaviour of the systems under study, in which a small change in the cause (the independent variable) can bring about a large quantitative or even qualitative change in the effect. As shown in Chapter 2 within the Neuronal Network approach, creative behaviour is also understood as a stochastic combinational process with unsystematic drifting; furthermore, it is chaotic and thus allows for the emergence of loosely connected new associations. All in all, there are important differences between the goals of Nonlinear Dynamical Systems Theory and those of the Neuronal Network approach. Nonlinear Dynamical Systems Theory accounts for how natural systems behave within stable states and how they qualitatively transfer from one stable state to the next. Neural networks, on the other hand, are data mining mathematical tools for capturing, analysing and classifying patterns.

One of the most essential aspects of Nonlinear Dynamical Systems Theory that is fundamentally linked to tactical creativity is multistability (Hristovski et al., 2011). Multistability is defined as the existence of more than one solution to a goal for the same set of constraint values (Edelman and Gally, 2001; Kelso, 1995). It is a genuine, nonlinear effect that naturally explains how a variety of tactical solutions (values of the collective variable) are generated for an identical set of constraint values (in the brain, brain-body-environment or a team system). This fact demonstrates that creativity is inevitably associated with the nonlinearity of the development of multiple action options (at an individual or team level). Linear systems generate only one solution for the same set of parameter values and therefore cannot account for creativity. In general, nonlinear interactions of system components are the fundamental mechanisms of qualitative natural changes. Creative products can be said to be exactly that – qualitatively novel products, unique compared to previous solutions.

With respect to what has been said above, the multistability of brain dynamics is particularly suitable for the explanation of the potential for tactical creativity in sports. In the last two decades there has been an increasing amount of data pointing to the nonlinear and hence multistable nature of the brain. Since nonlinearity is a consequence of the self-interaction of systems (e.g. brains, components), one may ask for the evidence of such properties in the brain. This evidence comes easily when one recalls the basic anatomical structure and structural organisation of the central nervous system. For instance, the reverberatory circuits at the neuronal level as well as reentrant complexes between large neuronal networks (Deco et al., 2008; Edelman and Gally, 2013) enable the self-interacting mechanisms that make multistability an inevitable outcome. Relevant decision making models at the brain level are also based on the notion of multistability (Brauna and Mattia, 2010; Deco et al., 2013). The search for dynamical mechanisms for decision making that may be structurally implemented in different ways within the CNS (e.g. reverberation, reentrant circuits, etc.) is one of the current hot topics in neuroscience.

Interestingly, Chow and colleagues (2007) suggest that the efficacy of the Teaching Games for Understanding approach could be explained as a constraints-led framework with its basis in Nonlinear Dynamical Systems Theory. The authors discuss motor learning processes with the view that the Nonlinear Dynamical Systems framework underpins the pedagogical methods of the Teaching Games for Understanding approach, demonstrating possible practical implementations in physical education.

Nonlinear Dynamical Systems Theory is one theoretical background for tactical creativity learning in team and racket sports, because some of its principles are closely related to the tactical creativity learning approach: both examine and describe complex processes in a complex environment, such as decision making in sports (for examples, see Chapter 5). In both learning approaches, recent advances in research and programmes carried out by researchers working in different fields of social and human science, e.g. psychology, sport science, movement science, and physiology, are important. A challenge in both research fields is found in the multiple degree-of-freedom actions made in uncertain environments by the players in team and racket sports where sudden changes in behaviour can often be observed. Key questions concern the meaningful information with which athletes are perceived to organise their solutions to a tactical problem, or the relation between the amount of information present in the performance environment and the tactical divergent thinking behaviour of children.

The implicit learning approach

For more than a century one main branch of psychology has been dealing with learning processes to help people undertake fast and effective training in order to understand and store new content in a more effective way (for a review, see Reber, 1993). Learning is expressed by the persistent modification of behaviour towards special stimuli or reactions due to previous experiences with similar stimuli or reactions (Domjan, 2008). Therefore, it is a process that creates relatively long-term changes in the behaviour potential of human beings as a result of experience. It is possible to differentiate between two learning processes, namely explicit and implicit learning, as demonstrated by an amount of research (for an overview see Cleeremans, Destrebecqz and Boyer, 1998).

Definitions (Reber, 1993)

Explicit learning relates to appropriation processes within intentional and target-oriented learning activities, which means the person "knows" that they are educated.

Implicit learning is an inductive process, through which knowledge is gained in such a way that neither the process of the knowledge acquisition, nor the gained knowledge, is part of conscious awareness.

Explicit learning is an intentional process which occurs consciously and the gained knowledge can usually be well verbalised. Therefore, a deliberate behaviour precedes the process of learning, which is influenced by an intentional, deliberate knowledge acquisition. In school, students learn most of the time in this manner, for example by learning vocabulary or playing instruments. The Teaching

Games for Understanding approach has to be characterised as an explicit learning approach in its second phase as well, since the teachers ask their students explicit questions. By doing so, the instructor requests that the students think about the game consciously. In contrast, babies learn how to walk without any explicit explanation of how this process works. Another example of implicit learning (IL) would be that human beings learn to speak their mother tongue correctly without being taught the grammar explicitly. In this type of casual, implicit learning, no verbalised cognitions are necessary about the reasons underlying the change in behaviour. Features of implicit learning also include that this learning: (1) occurs without capacity limitation, (2) results unconsciously ("learning without awareness"), (3) results in knowledge that is hard to verbalise, (4) follows incidental (casual) knowledge acquisition, (5) is unaffected by intention, (6) is less dependent on attention factors, and (7) is very stable in memory (e.g. bicycling, skiing).

In everyday life, both forms of learning play an important role. At this point, with reference to the TCA to be introduced later in this chapter, some empirical data on implicit learning, not only from sports, is presented below. To start with, the following experiment clearly demonstrates the effectiveness of implicit learning.

In the classic experiment by Reber (1967), subjects were requested to learn four hundred meaningless words by heart. During this learning phase, four-digit letter strings were presented that were created by an artificial grammar. This means that the subjects saw meaningless strings of consonants (e.g. PVPS), which followed a designated algorithm or system of rules that they were not aware of. After the learning phase, the participants were informed that the character strings they had just seen were the foundation of an artificial grammar. None of the participants were able to describe the artificial grammar. In the second test phase the subjects had to decide whether the presented character-string followed the grammar or not. They were supposed to categorize fifty new letter-strings as grammatically correct or incorrect. The result was impressive: the participants distinguished 69% of the letter-strings correctly. However, they were not able to specify or reflect the rules of the grammatical structure explicitly. In other words, they were not able to explain that their performance was a result of their own classification behaviour. Due to this observation and a variety of other, very similar studies, it was concluded that human beings are able to learn and use complex invariances and regularities from their environment without awareness or insight into the learning progress.

A variety of studies confirmed these results in other settings and learning environments (cf. Cleeremans et al., 1998). The methods used were similar in all experiments: the implicit learning participants were told that they should either learn something by heart or solve the task without any attention-demanding instructions, so that they did not learn anything consciously or search intentionally for commonalities. Only the tasks for the subjects varied. The aforementioned research includes sequencing rules for: reaction signals (Nissen and Bullemer, 1987; Cohen, Ivry and Keele, 1990), computer simulated control panels (Berry and Broadbent, 1988; Hayes and Broadbent, 1988) and the solution of motor tracking tasks (Magill and Hall, 1989; Magill, 1998).

There are also many similar studies in sports (e.g. Jackson & Farrow, 2005; Master, 1992; Master & Poolton, 2012; Maxwell, Masters, Kerr, & Weedon, 1991) that suggest that implicit learning is a powerful learning mechanism. For example, Raab (2003) examined implicit and explicit learned tactical decisions in basketball, handball and volleyball. A constructed if-then rule, conveyed by video scenes and in field experiments, was learned. The instructions differed between the implicit and explicit learning groups. The same video material was presented to the explicit group by verbally and visually instructed rules; they were instructed to apply rules for two hundred video scenes. The implicit group was instructed that the task would involve a memory test and that they should memorise the decisions of the predetermined player. In a volleyball scenario, twelve rules were determined regarding the point at which a setter should play to the five possible positions (three front and two back row players). The participants had to decide from which position the server would play which pass. Their decisions were presented by pinching a mat on the ground (A to D), from which they were supposed to throw a ball (cf. Figure 4.1) to a different number presented on the ceiling (1 to 6). In simple situations, visual implicitly presented information was enough for them to act effectively; however, compliance with explicit instructions led to distraction of attention and deterioration in performance.

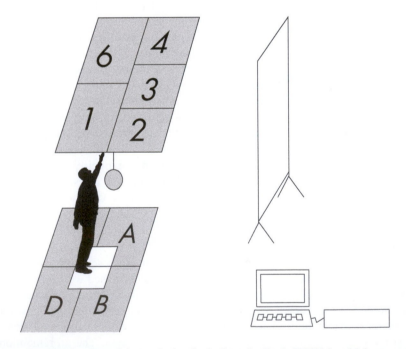

Figure 4.1 Construction of the tactical volleyball test by Raab (2003) in which one group learned through regulation specifications (explicit) and the other group passed a memory test (implicit)

The results in different team and racket sports were impressive and demonstrated that implicit learning is also verifiable for tactical rules. Implicit groups perform significantly better than explicit groups in the process of learning tactical rules. The implicit learners show long-term, stable learning effects but are able to verbalise the implicitly-learned if-then rules only vaguely.

How does implicit tactical learning work exactly? During the last few years, the interest in general learning mechanisms for perceptual-cognitive processes and motor sequences has increased steadily, particularly in the area of cognitive psychology (for a review, see Kunde, Koch and Hoffmann, 2004). The model by Hoffmann (2009) provides an explanatory and interesting approach to this learning.

Hoffmann (2009) concluded that human behaviour is controlled by effect anticipations, depending on the situational conditions (cf. Figure 4.2). For this purpose, we need to consider (effect anticipation) under which starting conditions (situational conditions) and determined invariant characteristics that determine behaviour (voluntary actions) lead to certain target situations with determined invariant characteristics (real effects) (see Figure 4.2).

Thus, connections between two serial situations can be formed continuously, as these situations will be experienced as consistently convertible into each other. For successful action control, behavioural acts (voluntary action) can be applied, which will enable a reliable transformation. Transferring this to team and racket sport situations, it could be concluded that the tactical solution of game situations can be described as the primary formation of action-effect associations or secondary contextualisation of action-effect associations. These connections are achieved by the consistent accomplishment of anticipated effects under consideration of the initial situational conditions with limited behavioural acts (some voluntary actions).

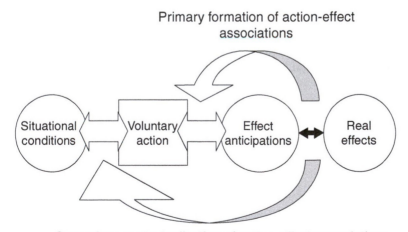

Primary formation of action-effect associations

Situational conditions — Voluntary action — Effect anticipations — Real effects

Secondary contextualization of action-effect associations

Figure 4.2 The acquisition of anticipative structures for the control of voluntary behaviour by Hoffmann (2009)

The fascinating thing about this learning mechanism is that the acquisition of certain connections happens incidentally, and therefore in an implicit manner. This is due to the fact that human beings have a need for predictability (Hoffmann, 2009). Another singularity of this model is that situations can be differentiated due to their usability. According to this, individuals learn how to differentiate situations from each other or to discover a situation's usability depending on their behaviour and intended effects, rather than a different (motor) behaviour. Children or beginners in a particular sport do not possess any sport experience. In other words, they have no special cognitive solution capability. Therefore, it is advisable at the start of a beginner's course to try to perceive situations in team and racket sports in a more global manner, and to solve them by using different motor embodiments. After acquiring this game-overlapping foundation in the form of the perception of different classes of situations, they may later arrive at a further differentiation of situations. In conclusion, it has to be said that the anticipative control of behaviour still enjoys a strong and worldwide research interest from the field of behavioural psychology as well as the areas of sports science and motor research (Hoffmann, 2010; Hoffmann et al., 2007). TCA is based on this implicit learning theory, which is discussed in more detail in the final part of this chapter.

Tactical transfer in team and raquet sports

"Intuitively it makes sense that the learning of one invasion game, perhaps football, might facilitate the learning of another invasion game, such as field hockey. Despite the different skills employed in these two games, they are very similar from a tactical perspective in which they both involve movements and skills aimed either at invading the opponent's space or at preventing them scoring by defending the space and the goal."

(Mitchell and Oslin, 1999, p. 162)

Our everyday experiences as well as our subjective perceptions on the field and in the gym seem to confirm that cognitive-tactical transfer can be monitored for a number of different children across a range of different team and racket sports. For example, when the cognitive competences develop that allow the identification of gaps in passing shots in tennis, these could also serve as the tactical realisation of a pass to the handball circle, or passes to the centre under the basket through free zones. However, in contrast to other fields of learning (e.g. computer technology: Beard, 1993; computer languages: Harvey and Anderson, 1996; reading and writing: McAloon, 1994; social competences: Toh and Woodnough, 1994; Tucker, 1996), there is only a number of limited studies in team and racket sports that have tried to substantiate cognitive-tactical transfer adaptations empirically (for a pedagogical motivation review, see Memmert and Harvey, 2010). As Mitchell and Oslin (1999, p. 163) said: "However, it appears that there have been no studies to investigate the extent to which knowledge and tactical understanding might transfer from performance of one game to the performance of another, leaving the curious to only speculate as to whether findings from research on motor skill transfer might also be applied to the notion of tactical transfer." In the following paragraphs, theoretical arguments for a positive effect of transfer are described first, followed by the presentation of empirical results.

Considering the outlined thoughts above from cognitive psychology (cf. Hoffmann, 2009), there are good reasons to assume the existence of positive tactical effects of transfer in team and racket sports. Tactical transfer performance in sports can be explained by psychological learning theories (cf. also Hoffmann, 2009). The basic approach of "common codings" developed by the working group of Wolfgang Prinz (see Elsner and Hommel, 2001; Hommel et al., 2002; Prinz, 1990, 1997) assumes that processes of perception and action control revert to a central level of representation (cf. Figure 4.3).

During common interactions, identical encoding exists for both mechanisms. This opinion presents a different view of the basic approach of separate encodings (e.g. sensory-motor transformation, see Hasbroucq and Guiard, 1991, p. 247). In this connection, mechanisms of impulse processing and action control are referred to as two separate functional systems. With the assumption of a collective representational medium, a "rule-based translation mechanism" is "spared" (interpreter). This is normally viewed as a connection between perception and action. An important characteristic to be considered at this distal level of representation is the complete commensurability of perception and action solutions.

Afferent structures represent objects and events in the outside world and are not seen as activity patterns in corresponding sensory organs. Compared to this, efferent structures represent intended motor actions as the result of the environment. These are not understood as activity patterns on associated effectors. Perceptive features and intentions for action are therefore commensurable due to their inseparable feature as the results of a common environment.

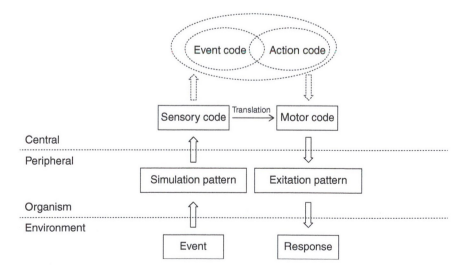

Figure 4.3 The "Common coding approach" in accordance with the theoretical framework outlined by Prinz (1997)

Different consequences may result from this "common coding approach" developed by Prinz (1990). For example, the initiation and implementation of actions is relieved by the fact that common features are available in the environment. Therefore, different characteristics of perception contents can define different characteristics of implementation at a cognitive level of representation. The result is that action plans (so-called action codes) are induced by sensory codes. This is postulated since the implementation of actions is controlled by the same representational structures, which serve the representation of perceptive contents.

For tactical-cognitive problem solving in team and racket sports, this means that the player achieves effects in his environment by motor action in specific situations. If technique is put on the same level as the competence of a player to resolve a situational task, it is illogical to separate technical and tactical training from each other. Therefore, motor skills are understood as a function to achieve specific, tactical goals. Without technique, no adequate tactics are possible. Without tactical knowledge, the use of different techniques will occur by chance (Hossner, 2001). For instance, French et al. (1996 a,b) and Graham et al. (1996) advised that games are as important as exercise for learning skills.

Many current, practical concepts in team and racket sports already consider the close and functional connection between tactical competence and technical execution (cf. Memmert and Roth, 2007; Griffin, Mitchell and Oslin, 1997). These concepts emphasise that it is appropriate to learn a technique in relation to specific situations and to offer less skill-oriented exercises. Based on these considerations, an array of different empirical evidence from sports science has been published in recent years.

The aim of the study by Mitchell and Oslin (1999) was to investigate the transfer of cognitive tactical decisions from badminton to pickleball in children aged fourteen to fifteen years. After the complex game skills in badminton were determined by the group's self-developed Game Performance Assessment Instrument (GPAI) in a twenty-minute game (pre-test), the children received a total of five hours of badminton-specific treatment. Based on the guidelines of the Tactical Awareness Approach and Teaching Games For Understanding (see Chapter 3) tactical competences like "setting up to attack", "defending space" and "recovery to centre court", as well as more general gaming behaviours, were trained. After re-assessment with the assistance of GPAI in a post-test, children were taught the same tactical competences for "pickleball" in a second learning phase. In the final transfer-test, the GPAI was employed again. The students only improved their skills during the first treatment; no improvement was shown for the pickleball unit. However, the tactical decision-making ability of the children was increased from post-test to transfer-test. This is initial evidence showing that acquired tactical competences in one game can be transferred to other similar game situations.

In a transfer study, Jones and Farrow (1999) investigated if tactical knowledge and competence from volleyball ("hand") could be transferred to badminton ("racket"). Two eighth grade classes successfully completed a four-week training programme in which volleyball-specific tactics were taught. A control group successfully completed a tactically orientated learning unit of the same length in a modification of rugby. In "touch rugby" the opponent must not be attacked physically – only a simple touch is allowed. Before and after the training session the decision quality, the required time for using tactical strategies, and the tactical knowledge of the students was surveyed in badminton doubles. The decision quality and tactical knowledge in badminton increased, whereas no increase in decision time was determined. For the volleyball intervention, the control rugby group did not show any changes for the three dependent variables. This finding suggests that tactical competences can be transferred to different team and racket sports with similar tactical aspects.

In a modified transfer study by Arend (1980, p. 14), the positive effect of "perception based pre-training" was confirmed. Previous perceptual experience in a structured environment entailed improvements in the motor solution of this situation. In an expertise study, Abernethy, Baker and Coté (2005) investigated the transfer of pattern recall skills from netball to basketball and to field hockey. They found that experts, in contrast to novices, showed positive transfer of pattern recall on defensive player positions, but not for pattern recall on offensive player positions (but see Gorman, Abernethy and Farrow, 2013).

In a big strand of research, the tactical transfer competences of children in different situations have been investigated several times (Memmert, 2004). In this research, several experimental designs were selected. These designs were partially interpreted by the so-called "path models". By doing so, the theoretical assumption that operations (cognitive-tactical solutions) can be used and acquired independently of the motor embodiment (e.g. hand, foot, racket) is always integrated. On the basis of theoretical considerations from Prinz (1990), the essential research question of an experimental transfer study in football (Memmert, 2004, Exp. 2) was whether solutions for a tactical task like support and orienting (which can be found across different team sports) can be developed, even though only football-specific training took place. For this purpose, tactical skills support and orienting were trained by offering game situations where children operated with their feet only. Results revealed a positive cognitive-tactical transfer effect from the "foot" to situations where children operate with hands or rackets. This provides support for the implications of the models of human behaviour developed by Hoffmann (2009).

These results confirm the observations of Speelmann and Kirsner (1997, p. 100) that "mechanisms underlying skill acquisition would appear to be adaptive to the nature of the environment rather than fixed and only responsive to particular environments". The solutions to basic tactical tasks, which are applicable later in team and racket sport, can be formed during the training of only one motor embodiment. For instance, when children need to act with their feet in situations of running free, they have to develop cognitive mechanisms for solutions in spatial perception and decisions similar to tasks where hands or a racket are used. Therefore, the task of the trainer is clearly to prepare the children for the identification of spatial and temporal patterns or basic conditions of the environment so that they can quickly show adequate cognitive and motor skills on their own (e.g. football) or in other sporting tasks (e.g. hockey).

"Recent literature related to game teaching has looked carefully at using tactical approaches and has suggested that numerous research questions remain unanswered (Rink, French and Graham, 1996). One such question relates to the transfer of learning from one game to another within the same tactical category" (Mitchell and Oslin, 1999, p. 162). In the year 2014, a variety of empirical research shows clear tactical transfer effects across team and racket sports.

Variability makes the difference!

Recent research in motor learning supports the important link between cognitive processes, such as attention or perception, and motor skill acquisition (cf. Sherwood and Lee, 2003). Many motor skills in sports consist of both cognitive and motor factors within a complex interaction (Starkes and Allard, 1993). This view is also supported by the theoretical frameworks of Prinz (1997) and Hoffmann (2009). Different kinds of methods have been investigated in recent years to enhance the learning of complex skills in sports. Current motor approaches, such as those supporting random motor learning, contain cognitive explanatory mechanisms (e.g. the level-of-processing approach, Lee, 1988). A wide variety of basic approaches in motor skills research propagate the notion that variable learning has substantial positive effects on learning, automatising and stabilising motor skills, in contrast to monotonous learning (cf. Memmert, Hagemann, Althoetmar, Geppert and Seiler, 2009). Three important research programmes developed methodological principles such as the "Variability of Practice Hypothesis" proposed by Schmidt (1975), the "Context Interference Approach" put forward by Battig (1966) and the "Differential Learning Approach" of Schöllhorn, Hegen and Davids (2012), which will be discussed next in more detail and with emphasis on a link to more perceptual, cognitive-tactical learning in team and racket sports.

Variability of practice hypothesis

One of the most widely examined phenomena in motor learning in recent years has been the variability of practice hypothesis (for a review see Shea & Wulf, 2005). A considerable amount of research has indicated that a wide range of parameter variability (e.g. movement velocity, muscle force, limb angles) introduced through variable training is more effective for parameter learning in complex motor skills than constant, drill and practice methods (cf. Memmert, 2006b; Moxley, 1979; Shea and Kohl, 1991; Wulf, 1991; Schmidt, 2003).

For example, Memmert (2006b) analysed the long-term effects of practical schedule on shooting performance in basketball during real field training. Thirty-two college students completed voluntary basketball training sessions in one of two equal-sized groups, experiencing constant versus random training. The constant training group took 160 shots from the free throw line, while the variable practice group took 160 shots from different positions around the restricted area. Participants completed a pre- and post-test from the free throw line, and one year later, they completed a retention test without knowing in advance that they would be tested again after one year. Results showed considerable learning and transfer improvements in both training groups at all measurement times. While the constant training group revealed better acquisition, the random training group revealed better retention (see Figure 4.4). Therefore, results indicate that a variable sport-specific training programme produces long-term learning effects in addition to those usually found with short-term retention intervals (see Lee, Magill and Weeks, 1985). In summary, the variability of practice hypothesis suggests that variable practice-oriented sport training programmes produce better short- and long-term learning effects for complex sport skills than constant training programmes.

In the perceptual-cognitive domain, there are only a few studies that show the powerful effects of variable learning. For example, Memmert et al. (2009) investigated a general rule in both practical motor and perceptual training states that improved learning performance by presenting simple tasks first, followed by more difficult tasks (cf. Schmidt and Wrisberg, 2004). One traditional learning rule in motor skill acquisition is that easy training conditions should be incorporated first into the motor learning process (Čoh, Jovanović-Golubović and Bratić, 2004) for beginners, followed later by more difficult tasks. The results reported by Memmert and colleagues demonstrated that in perceptual learning the *Easy-to-Hard* principle is not superior to a random one. On the contrary, the mean values of the groups in the post-test and the retention test actually suggested that a random perceptual training group has an advantage. The authors concluded that it is not always helpful to reduce the difficulty level of the task for learners. A

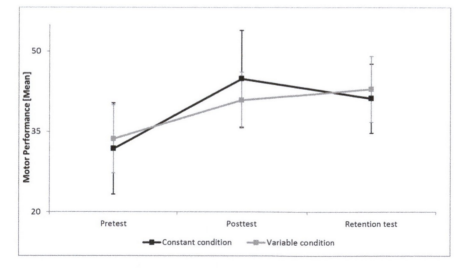

Figure 4.4 Learning performance (means and standard deviations) in the two training groups at all measurement times

combination of simple and difficult tasks could present a stimulating learning environment and stronger preoccupation with the object of learning (cf. Lee, 1988; Magill and Hall, 1990; Shea and Morgan, 1979; Shea and Zimny, 1983).

Context-interference approach

A second central approach in human movement science stems from context interference effects. Shea and Morgan (1979) and Shea and Zimny (1983) assumed that under contextual interference, the more difficult a task is, the larger the required information processing effort (elaboration benefit explanation). As such, increasingly separate memory representations are used by elaboration processes (e.g. multiple encoding), which is ultimately reflected in an increased retention stability. Conversely, Lee, Magill and Weeks (1983) saw the decisive advantage of random practice quite differently. Constantly changing tasks under random conditions lead to processes of forgetting, which have to be compensated by cognitive effort. In contrast to blocked order, in which the same action plan can always be used, the tasks are constantly changed in a random order so that the action plan has to be reconstructed (action plan reconstruction view). This permanent cognitive reconstruction process is seen as the reason for the increased retention stability. Both theoretical approaches clarify that under random conditions, and even in perceptual learning, the processing conditions can be made more difficult, thereby learning is accelerated. Through the influence of feedback reminders in random practice, it was possible to show that the learning advantages frequently found in random, as opposed to blocked, practice could be destroyed.

For some time now, motor learning has been concerned with context interference effects (for a review, see Magill and Hall, 1990). As shown in Figure 4.5, these effects concern the fact that practicing tasks in a random order leads to lower acquisition and higher retention than practicing tasks in a blocked order (Shea and Morgan, 1979). This context interference effect was replicated, generalised and extended to sports in numerous follow-up experiments (Gabriele, Lee and Hall, 1991; Goode and Magill, 1986; Hall and Magill, 1995; Lee, Magill and Weeks, 1985; Shea, Kohl and Indermill, 1990; Sherwood, 1996; Wrisberg, 1991; Wrisberg and Liu, 1991; Young, Cohen and Husak, 1993).

Memmert et al. (2009) were the first to attempt to replicate context interference effects in more perceptual skills, such as anticipating the direction of an opponent's stroke. In this study, forty-one college students were assigned to one of two groups: two blocked perceptual training groups, and random perceptual training at a computer with either a random temporal or a blocked temporal video sequence. The results showed significant improvements in both training groups. The random perceptual training group showed a significant advantage compared to one blocked perceptual training group (but not the others). Therefore, context interference effects may only partly be replicated in perceptual skill learning. Descriptively, at no stage are the perceptual performances of both blocked training groups better than those of the random training group. Based on these findings, it was interpreted that the context interference effects (poorer learning performance, improved

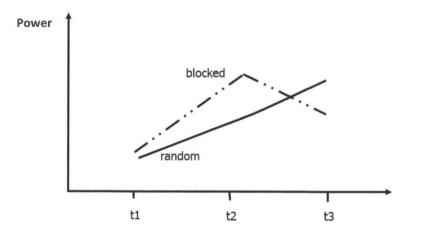

Figure 4.5 The typical context interference effects: practicing tasks in random order leads to lower acquisition and higher retention than practicing tasks in a blocked order

retention performance) could be a possibility for perceptual learning skills in team and racket sports.

The differential learning approach

The idea of differential learning (for a recent reference, see Schöllhorn, Hegen and Davids, 2012) in the area of motor skills learning should at this point be taken as an illustration that this type of learning is related to a diversification in tactical and creative learning.

Building on contemporary, non-linear dynamical system theories (e.g. Haken et al., 1985; for an overview, see Schöllhorn et al., 2012; see also this chapter), Wolfgang Schöllhorn developed the method of differential practice. The central point of his theory is that the biggest steps in the learning process are achieved when the organism has to newly adapt to given situations (Savelsbergh, Kamper, Rabius, De Koning and Schöllhorn, 2010).

Motor variability is necessary since two identical initial situations rarely exist in team and racket sports. For example, the number of participants, the pace, the distances between teammates and opponents, the ground, the weather or further cognitive factors (e.g. score, point in game, influence of spectators) vary continuously and have an influence on the motor system. With this method of differential learning, the stereotype of the repetition of an ideal (set point value), oriented movement in terms of the "loop-in" of the optimal motion sequence, is not displayed in the foreground, but the variable practice is. Both at the beginning of the learning process as well as in the later optimisation of the technical motion sequence of an expert, this method introduces new possibilities for the improvement of training and economisation. Differential learning includes the targeted application of different motion sequences with a large deviation from the later performed "ideal" movement, and avoids repetition of "identical" motion sequences.

Differential learning:

While machines rarely make mistakes but are not yet completely able to learn complex strategies, human beings can never perform two identical movements, but they are astonishingly able to cope with new situations. Despite this fact, the impression exists that most traditional training programmes persistently ignore these characteristics, because they are oriented towards methodical rules, utilising "practice-practice-practice" (criterion: number of repetitions) as well as the "loop-in" (criterion: reduction of degrees of freedom) of movements. Originating from a dynamical system approach, Schöllhorn and colleagues (cf. Schöllhorn, Hegen and Davids, 2012; Schöllhorn et al., 2006) introduce the concept of differential learning, which emphasises alternation and fluctuation as meaningful components of the learning process and demand that these should be explicitly supported in training programmes. Therefore, mistakes are important for the athlete in order to sufficiently develop individual interpolation mechanisms and self-organising processes, which again are necessary so he can react appropriately to unfamiliar situations.

Beckmann, Winkel and Schöllhorn (2010) were able to demonstrate that differential learning does not only lead to a bigger increase in performance (greater rates of learning), but also to more stable learning (greater retention) in comparison to the traditional learning methods. Differential training programmes implement three methodological principles:

- "individuality": since the same competition results can be achieved with different techniques (cf. Schöllhorn, Hegen and Davids, 2012), the existence of an ideal technique and its trainability is put into question.
- "repetition without repetition": exercises are normally not repeated, which means that the conscious implementation of two identical movements should be avoided (Schöllhorn, Michelbrink, Welminski and Davids, 2009).
- "maximal variation": in the language of the schema theory of Schmidt (1975), the invariants and parameters of the motion sequence to be learned are systematically changed (see this Chapter, Variability).

Another advantage of differential learning can also be seen in the unconscious, permanent adaption of movement to the constantly changing conditional qualifications of the athlete (Frank, Michelbrink, Beckmann, & Schöllhorn, 2008). The adaption to the constantly changing determining factors of the movement through differential learning provides the chance to also integrate the adaption to physical changes due to conditional training content or due to the development of limited increases in length and mass. The higher affectivity of this method can be justified by the fact that the repeated presentation of a constant stimulus can lead to a decrease of adaptation by the learner through the reduction of absorbed information (see Schöllhorn et al., 2012). The greater effectiveness of the differential learning approach is objectified by the measurement of so-called "stochastic resonance": the higher the resonance is, the more distinct the adaptation towards the learning performance. That means that differential coordination training is repetition without repetition.

For practical experience, the model of differential learning means that technical-coordinative learning can be optimised by maximal variation of the initial situation as well as by the highest possible individualisation (cognitive and motor qualifications). Due to consistent adaption to new environments, movements can be effectuated. By doing so, sensory processes for the realisation of motor movements (e.g. passing under time pressure) are especially in demand. Meanwhile, Schöllhorn has carried out a considerable number of empirical studies that clarified the notable advantages of differential training compared to traditional training (for a review, see Schöllhorn et al., 2012). In a nutshell, the differential learning approach leads to a bigger increase in performance during the same scope of training, and shows the same increase in a shorter time. Therefore, this method should especially be observed in the learning process of beginners, but also in top athletes.

Cautiously – quasi vice versa – it can be concluded that it is not only creative cognitive behaviour that can be learned through diversification; motor skills can also be learned through the variable environment to develop faster and more variably.

Teaching model of the tactical creativity approach

In this and the next chapter a theoretical framework (tactical creativity approach, TCA, see Figure 4.6) is proposed based on more than twenty individual experiments, intended to provide the basis for the development of tactical creativity in team and racket sports for children, youth and professionals. The component model by Sternberg and Lubart (1991; see Chapter 2) with the factors such as attention, expertise, environment, personality, and motivation, together with the dynamical system approach, the implicit learning approach, tactical transfer research, and the importance of variability, all provide the theoretical framework for the TCA (see Figure 4.6) and for the individual studies which we have conducted over the last thirteen years (see also Memmert, 2010c, 2011). Note here that variability and all the components of the Sternberg model also play a key role in a constraints-led perspective (Davids et al., 2008).

From an ecological dynamics point of view, *control parameters* such as the degree of movement variability are defined as informational variables that can guide a system between different states of organisation, whereas *order parameters* are defined as collective variables that describe the organisation of such systems (cf. Araújo, Davids and Hristovski, 2006). Control parameters are mathematical

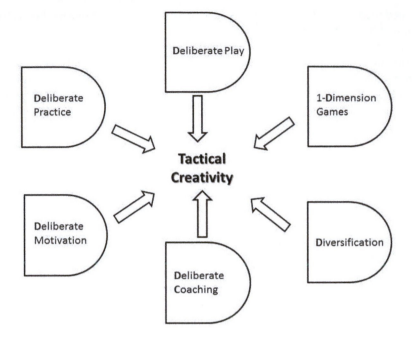

Figure 4.6 Theoretical framework of the Tactical Creativity Approach (TCA): The six **Ds** fostering tactical creativity in team and racket sports. The order of the six principles indicates a chronological order from children and youth training to adolescence and adult training. While the first four principles (starting with Deliberate Play) are more suitable for younger age groups, all principles are useful for groups at an older age and should be integrated in training units

representations of the constraints (or their combinations) that act on biological movement or social systems. According to the scale of the system under research, parameters can be defined on an individual or team level. These can either be nonspecific (e.g. constraints that have a distinct informational nature from movement (generally behavioural) characteristics) or specific (e.g. constraints which have the same informational nature as movement (generally behavioral) characteristics). The specific constraints always refer directly to the behaviour under scrutiny.

The order parameter (e.g. the collective variable) captures the collective cooperative behaviour of the player's (or team's) components (e.g. degrees of freedom) and serves two roles. First, it informs the components of the players in action (e.g. the attacker or a team) how to behave cooperatively, and second, it informs the perceiver (e.g. the defender) about the mode of action to be taken by the attacker. This is the reason why the order parameter or the collective variable may also be called the *informator* (Haken, 2000). Hence, the collective variable defined on either the individual or the team level gives information about the behavioural structure and the coordination patterns that are created under certain constraints. Respective tactical solutions are the temporary stable values of the collective variable or the informator.

The collective variable plays another crucial role because it causally constrains the component behaviours that form it (Hristovski et al., 2011). This is Haken's slaving principle, formally given as a centre manifold theorem. Components are subordinated to the collective variable, creating another circular causality. Components form the collective behaviour through their interactions, but this collective behaviour then subordinates the components, suggesting the natural emergence of a two-level hierarchy. On a more practical level, individual players move in a certain way guided by the information intake (interaction), thus forming a macroscopic behavioural pattern. Nevertheless, this macroscopic behavioural pattern does not allow for individual players to conduct any imaginable action individually (Hristovski et al., 2011). For example, if a defensive line in a football team is supposed to form a compact back-four belt, individual players cannot simply pass the ball to any given place. The belt formation (collective variable) constrains their individual possibilities. Clearly, the collective variable enhances or suppresses the number of action opportunities, and this can generate more variable and original solutions.

Hence, the TCA attempts to connect these two informational variables, namely control parameters and collective variables. The notion of information as a sense of affordance is different to the concept of information as collective variables given as informational entropy (Hristovski et al., 2009). The point is that ecological perceptual information of affordances generates a number of action opportunities; the number of action opportunities is quantified as information entropy. The information entropy may change abruptly with changea of the control parameter (a set of constraints), but also continuously as a consequence of changes in the probabilities of action, which leads to a change of the ecological information, i.e. the perception of different number or type of affordances (Hristovski et al., 2009).

In other words, affordances, once picked up, can inform the attacker's perceptual systems about the environmental structure (e.g. gaps in the defense) and thus constrain the order parameter (i.e. the number of action modes and their probabilities) for these attackers. This in turn generates information for the defensive players about the macroscopic behaviour of the attacking players. Guided by this information, defenders change their activities and hence change the number of opportunities of action (affordances) for the attackers. The emergence of novel, creative information in tactical solution situations is dependent on the changing constraints (specifically tactical constraints), and can influence the dynamics of actions in team and racket sport situations. This is the basis for the **Deliberate Play** and **Deliberate Practice** principles of the TCA (see Figure 4.6), which state that children should act in relatively uninstructed game forms which include sudden changes of environment. In further learning processes the units should become more and more structured with the main focus on effectively fostering sport-specific individual performance.

The second of the informational variables, named the collective variable (order parameter or informator), is important for (tactical) decision-making since it is the order parameter of the action mode that informs when the decision is made by the player. Nonlinear Dynamical Systems research on decision making focuses on the context in which the actions arise. For example, it has been shown that for certain contexts the number of opportunities for action, i.e. the diversity of actions, can be maximised (Hristovski et al., 2006). This context is defined by environmental, personal, as well as task constraints (Newell, 1986) and can offer many possible higher level constraints that modify the processes of decision making, action selection, and action control in humans. This context-dependent characteristic is a dominant part of the tactical creativity learning approach and stresses the coupling of the organism, its perception, cognition, and action with its environment. In this respect, the dynamical approach can be juxtaposed with the tactical creativity learning approach since the main methodological characteristic of the latter is an emphasis on the exact and systematic change of the environment for the learning of behaviour and action in humans. Therefore, we need natural environments with clear constraints. As argued in the discussion of tactical transfer in team and racket sports, this view is also supported by state-of-the-art psychological theories including the Common Coding approach (Prinz, 1997) or the Anticipation Model (Hoffmann, 2009).

I chose the term 1-**D**imension-Games in the TCA (see Figure 4.6) to indicate that fostering tactical creativity requires the integration of error learning, implicit learning, and some aspects of differential learning within the same concept; of course, these learning mechanisms are also involved in **D**eliberate Play. Therefore, 1-**D**imension-Games offer the learner tactical understanding without repetition, and self-organised and engaged acting in complex and random learning environments. Here, nonlinear interaction can be defined as a kind of self-interaction. Player A's action changes player B's actions, which in turn have an influence on player A's consecutive action. This circumstance – the action of player A changing itself by changing the action of player B – is called co-adaptivity or circular causality. Through this mechanism, player A's action may self-suppress or self-enhance depending on whether or not it enabled a good condition for player B's actions, who can be unrelated to a teammate or an opponent. This can be generalised to higher numbers of players, too, where each one's action changes others' decisions (players B, C, D, etc.) and these in turn change the actions of the other players. As described before in the first sub-section of Chapter 4, regarding the non-linear dynamic system approach, the basis of creativity is multistability, and the basis of multistability is nonlinearity (Hristovski et al., 2011).

Another important factor in Nonlinear Dynamical Systems Theory is intention, which is defined as a specific constraint that can impose particular intended directional or timing behaviours on a desired movement pattern (Kelso, 1995). Depending on the context, some intentions form and other dissolve. An important example of specific constraints on biological movement is task constraints. In nonlinear dynamical systems, unlike anything in the linear characterisation of movement systems, a minute change in the value of a control parameter can bring about a drastic qualitative change in a movement system's dynamics. For example, in football, a supposedly small change in a control parameter can lead to the emergence of a new type of system organisation – for instance, an innovative type of technical pass as a solution in specific tactical midfield situations, or a novel tactical formation in a counter-attack. This event is called a phase transition in the system's dynamics, and is related to the spontaneous self-organisation degrees of freedom of the motor system (or team) (Hristovski, Davids and Araujo, 2009). This spontaneous change is a result of the loss of the stability of a previous state of organisation (e.g. an original action) and not a consequence of some specific agent prescribing the change. Therefore, it is of particular interest in movement and sport science to uncover the influential (i.e. perceptual, psychological, morphological, environmental or task) constraints. These assumptions fit well with the "Variability of Practice Hypothesis" developed by Schmidt (1975), the "Context-Interference-Approach" of Battig (1966) and the "Differential Learning Approach" by Schöllhorn, Hegen and Davids (2012), highlighting that variability, per se, is extremely important for motor, perception, and cognitive learning. This is also precisely the goal of **D**iversification (see Figure 4.6): to request the students to unconsciously come up with new ideas and solutions for different situations in a variety of embodiments, such as the hands, feet, hockey sticks or tennis rackets. Thus, the principle of the TCA **D**iversification goes beyond current learning approaches like the "Variability of Practice Hypothesis" or the "Context Interference Approach". While motor learning models distinguish a difference between variability within a movement or action class, **D**iversification stresses variability between action and movement classes. Chapter 5 will discuss empirical evidence concerning how tactical creativity can be fostered using 1-**D**imension-Games. In addition, basic tactical tasks in general, and particularly in football, are described.

Based on the component model by Sternberg and Lubart (1991), attention and motivation are two further factors that have positive effects on general creativity. Therefore, coaching strategies and methodical principles for conducting training units become more and more important (see Chapter 5 for a more detailed discussion). Attention and focus in team and racket sports (**D**eliberate Coaching, see Figure 4.6) can be manipulated especially through certain instruction options and by giving external implicit information impulses. With a broad attention focus, unexpected and potentially better alternative solutions can be perceived, used, and hence learned. It is also possible to consider instructions that cause certain motivational moods in children (**D**eliberate Motivation, see Figure 4.6). This is another connection between the TCA and the non-linear dynamic system approach. A broader attention focus and mood belong to the class of personal constraints within the constraints-led perspective (Davids et al., 2008). For instance, a wider attention focus may lead to the detection and online tracking of a broader set of affordances. Thus, this can lead to more opportunities for specific actions.

Finally, these **D**s will help to develop a wide range of game forms for teaching and coaching tactical creativity in physical education that can be useful guidelines for lecturing staff, students, teachers and coaches. In order to generate decision possibilities and original solutions, a player must be able to perceive all the pertinent information from his/her environment (e.g. the position of teammates and opponents, players emerging unexpectedly etc.) and take it into account in his/her action plan. Creative football or basketball players set themselves apart by perceiving opportunities in the game as they emerge. For example, a creative player may intend to pass the ball to player B, but she perceives at the last moment that player C is suddenly unmarked and in a better position, and therefore makes the decision to pass the ball to her instead.

Summary

In this chapter different kinds of learning approaches are described that are important for the Tactical Creativity Approach (TCA). The first purpose of this chapter was to build a bridge between the research concerning tactical creativity and the non-linear dynamical system approach (e.g. Davids et al., 2008). Nonlinear Dynamical Systems Theory defines control parameters as informational variables that can guide a system between different organisation states. In addition, order parameters are defined as collective variables that describe the organisation of such systems. Nonlinear Dynamical Systems Theory focuses more on qualitative changes in the system, which makes it similar to the qualitative neuronal network approach explained in Chapter 2. Because of the importance of task constraints, small changes in the value of a control parameter can bring about a radical qualitative change in a player system's dynamics. Nonlinear (self) interactions lead to multistability, and this creates multiple options that may provoke creative tactical solutions (Hristovski et al., 2011).

Research from psychology and sport psychology demonstrates that implicit learning (e.g. Cleeremans et al., 1998; Reber, 1993) is a powerful learning mechanism that is important for different kinds of learning activities (e.g. **D**eliberate Play) and coaching strategies (**D**eliberate Coaching), not only in sport. Furthermore, the model developed by Hoffmann (2009) is able to explain tactical-cognitive transfer effects, which we pick up again later in the TCA term **D**iversification. In addition, we introduced the "Variability of Practice Hypothesis" by Schmidt (1975), the "Context-Interference-Approach" by Battig (1966) and the "Differential Learning Approach" by Schöllhorn et al. (2012), which demonstrate that variability is important for motor, perception, and cognitive skill learning. This will become important in the TCA regarding the principle of **D**eliberate Play. Finally, based on the component model by Sternberg and Lubart (1991), we introduced a theoretical framework with six **D**s that may foster tactical creativity. The empirical evidence and the recommendations will be described in more depth in the following chapters.

Discussion questions

1   Explain the dynamical system approach in connection with the tactical creativity approach.
2   Try to give some practical examples that show the importance of the nonlinear dynamical systems theory in team and racket sport.
3   Give some examples of everyday life activities that show the importance of implicit learning.

4 What are the differences and what are the similarities between the Teaching Games for Understanding approach and an implicit learning approach for the development of game sense?

5 What is meant by tactical transfer in team and racket sports, and how can one use this idea in practical training sessions?

6 Discuss the "Variability of Practice Hypothesis" in relation to motor skill learning in team and racket sports.

7 Discuss the "Context-Interference-Approach" in relation to motor skill learning in team and racket sports.

8 Discuss the "Differential Learning Approach" in relation to to motor skill learning in team and racket sports.

9 Describe the three macro rules concerning environmental conditions for developing tactical creativity in young children.

10 Describe the three micro rules concerning training conditions for developing tactical creativity in young children.

Additional reading

Araújo, D., Davids, K. & Serpa, S. (2005) An ecological approach to expertise effects in decision-making in a simulated sailing regatta. *Psychology of Sport and Exercise*, 6, 671–692.

Hoffmann, J. (2009) ABC: A Psychological Theory of Anticipative Behavioral Control. In G. Pezzulo, M.V. Butz, O. Sigaud & G. Baldassarre (eds.): *Anticipatory Behaviour in Adaptive Learning Systems. From Psychological Theories to Artificial Cognitive Systems* (pp. 10–30). Heidelberg: Springer.

Hoffmann, J., Berner, M., Butz, M.V., Herbort, O., Kiesel, A., Kunde, W. & Lenhard, A. (2007) Explorations of Anticipatory Behavioral Control (ABC): A report from the Cognitive Psychology Unit of the University of Würzburg. *Cognitive Processing*, 8, 133–142.

Memmert, D. (2010c) Development of Creativity in the Scope of the TGfU Approach. In J.I. Butler & L.L.Griffin (eds.), *Teaching Games for Understanding: Theory, Research and Practice* (Second Edition) (pp. 231–244). Champaign: Human Kinetics.

Memmert D. (2011) Sports and Creativity. In M.A. Runco and S.R. Pritzker (eds.), *Encyclopedia of Creativity* (Second Edition), vol. 2 (pp. 373–378). San Diego: Academic Press.

Memmert, D., Hagemann, H., Althoetmar, R. Geppert, S. & Seiler, D. (2009) Conditions of practice in perceptual skill learning. *Research Quarterly for Exercise and Sport*, 80, 32–43.

Prinz, W. (1997) Perception and action planning. *European Journal for Cognitive Psychology*, 9, 129–168.

Prinz, W. & Hommel, B. (eds.) (2002) *Common Mechanisms in Perception and Action: Attention and performance XIX*. Oxford: Oxford University Press.

Schöllhorn, W., Michelbrink, M., Beckmann, H., Trockel, M., Sechelmann, M. & Davids, K. (2006) Does noise provide a basis for the unification of motor learning theories? *International Journal of Sport Psychology*, 37, 1–21.

Shea, C. H. & Wulf, G. (2005) Schema theory: A critical appraisal and reevaluation. *Journal of Motor Behaviour*, 37, 85–101.

5   Empirical evidence for the tactical creativity approach in team and racket sports

My theoretical assumptions were summarised in the Tactical Creativity Approach (see Figure 4.6) in Chapter 4. All the six **D**s are methodological accents in respective training units that can be steered by teachers or coaches. They shed light on the processes that can play a role in the development of creative performances. In Chapter 5 I will give empirical evidence for the six **D**s in developing tactical creativity in young children: **D**eliberate Play, 1-**D**imension Games, **D**iversification, **D**eliberate Coaching, **D**eliberate Motivation, and **D**eliberate Practice. The focus will be on 1-**D**imensional Games and **D**eliberate Coaching, since these are relatively new concepts which can be connected to other attention paradigms (the common coding approach, the inattentional blindness paradigm, breadth of attention) and since a substantiated amount of empirical proof for these dimensions can be given. In addition, the focus will also be on **D**iversification since this is a relatively new methical rule that can be discussed in context with other paradigms (the context interference paradigm, the differential learning paradigm, variability) and initial empirical evidence can be presented.

All in all, the reported research does not provide an isolated analysis of relevant cognitive processes such as attention, which are responsible for the accomplishment of creative solutions especially in team and racket sports, but also attempts to emphasise the search for further complex correlation patterns between all the resources, such as expertise and attention.

Tactical creativity and deliberate play

Côté, Baker and Abernethy (2007) proposed four different kinds of playing characteristics for children to learn tactical and technical skills: Free Play, Deliberate Play, Structured Practice, and Deliberate Practice. From a methodological point of view in TCA, two ways of training (Côté et al., 2007) can be distinguished based on scientific evidence regarding the development of tactical creativity (cf. Memmet et al., 2010): the term "Deliberate Play" refers to non-instructed involvement in play-oriented and at-first-sight unstructured activities in the absence of coaching and feedback. "Deliberate Practice", however, offers targeted and task-centred training programmes based on careful instructions and detailed and immediate feedback (see the last sub-section in this Chapter).

Definition (Côté, et al. 2007)

- "Deliberate Play": uninstructed and free operation in game oriented, unstructured situations.
- "Deliberate Practice": instructionalised operation in routine-centred, structured situations with the aim of effectively improving specific individual performance criteria.

As Côté and Hay (2002) suggested, the sampling years (ages seven to twelve) are characterised by a high frequency of Deliberate Play. The self-determination theory and Vallerand's hierarchical model of motivation in sports support the notion that early Deliberate Play will have a positive effect on intrinsic motivation over time (cf. Ryan and Deci, 2000; Vallerand, 2001). Particularly for beginners, only small games can provide the framework within which children can gather new experiences. In addition, a significant amount of research in relation to context-interference effects, especially variability and random training, also supports this view (see Chapter 4).

Since the aforementioned treatment study (Memmert and Roth, 2007) also showed positive effects of specific training concepts, the role of different forms of sport involvement and practice conditions of highly creative and less creative team sport athletes were contrasted in a movement biography study by Memmert, Baker and Bertsch (2010). Twelve coaches carefully selected the most and least creative players from their teams (football, basketball, field hockey, and team handball). These data, presented in Figure 5.1, showed that unstructured

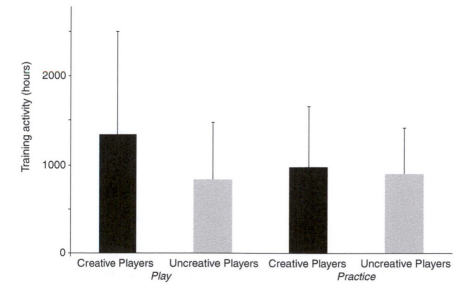

Figure 5.1 Amount of training activity as a function of creativity (creative vs. non-creative player) and training structure (practice vs. play)

play-like involvement (Côté, Baker and Abernethy, 2003) plays a crucial role in the development of creative behaviour in basketball, handball, field hockey and football.

Through an experimental study in basketball, Greco, Memmert, and Morales (2010) investigated a Deliberate Play training programme in more depth. In this field-based investigation, youth basketball players aged ten to twelve years completed two different kinds of basketball training. While the Deliberate Play group operated in relatively unstructured majority/minority situations (1x2, 2x3 and 3x4) or situations with a neutral player (1x1+1, 2x2+1, 3x3+1 and 4x4+1) most of the time, the placebo group practiced traditional, basketball-specific routines according to precise guidelines (Lumsden, 2001). To be more concrete, the Deliberate Play training groups spent 591 minutes (58.8%) in unstructured game forms and the placebo group spent significantly less: 271 minutes (23.3%). In contrast, the placebo training group spent significantly more time (493 minutes; 42.3%) in structured game forms and the Deliberate Play groups spent only 72.5 minutes (7.2%). No significant differences were observed in conversation with the coach (about 20%, respectively), training competition (about 15%, respectively), or total training time (about 1050 minutes, respectively). Tactical creativity with Game Test Situations (see Chapter 6) was assessed before and after an eighteen-lesson intervention.

The aforementioned study demonstrated that the Deliberate Play training programme leads to greater improvements in both convergent and divergent tactical thinking than in the training of a control group (see Figure 5.2). Further empirical research is necessary to find out whether creativity is trainable in the later stages of a player's development, e.g. using adult training scenarios.

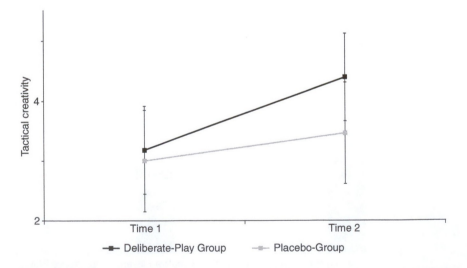

Figure 5.2 Ratings of training performance in tactical creativity: Means and standard deviations for two training groups at both measurement times

Tactical creativity and 1-dimension games

Recently the term "small-sided games" has become more and more popular, which is evident in the publications of the first review articles on this topic (Hill-Haas, Dawson, Impellizzeri and Coutts, 2011; Clemente, Couceiro, Martins and Mendes, 2012). Small-sided games are defined as adaptations of real matches, reducing the game complexity into small parts, e.g. being played on reduced pitch areas, using modified rules and involving a smaller number of players (e.g. Clemente et al., 2012; Hill-Haas et al., 2011; Rampinini et al., 2006). According to the literature, these modified games are generally used by trainers to develop technical skills or aerobic fitness components (Gabbett, 2006; Gabbett, Jenkins and Abernethy, 2009), and are mainly utilised in football or basketball (Hill-Haas, Coutts, Rowsell and Dawson, 2008; Hill-Haas, Dawson, Coutts and Rowsell, 2009).

The main differences between small-sided games and the 1-**D**imension Games, which we introduced in this chapter, are that 1-**D**imension Games: (1) promote the development of tactical components; (2) encourage players to find creative solutions; and (3) have a structure that is easy to change in order to apply the technique to different team and racket sports which have a non-specific format. These criteria will be explained in more detail below.

1-**D**imension Games are simple game forms that foster tactical creativity. They have clearly defined game ideas, fixed numbers of players, and defined rules and environmental conditions. Hence, the main idea is based on fundamental constellations with clearly allocated roles in order to create recurring and consistent conditions with many repetitions for children. That follows the differential learning idea: repetition without repetition. Memmert and Roth (2007) as well as Memmert (2007) showed that the tactical creativity of children can be improved best with 1-**D**imension Games.

1-**D**imension Games train individual basic tactical components through a high number of repeated similar situation constellations (see the following sections for examples in team and racket sports and football). This is the main difference between 1-**D**imension Games and the traditional games or game forms, in which different kinds of tactical abilities are necessary to play the game successfully. 1-**D**imension Games can be characterised by their (Memmert, 2007; Memmert and Roth, 2007):

- focus on *one* basic tactical component
- specification of obvious role allocation
- specification of certain real-world situations in team and racket sports
- guarantee of always returning realistic situations
- guarantee of constant realistic situations
- guarantee of high numbers of repetitions
- guarantee of different team-mates and opponents by systematic rotation
- guarantee of repetition of tactical tasks without repetition of the exact same tactical tasks

The main aim of 1-**D**imension Games is that children learn in complex and dynamic situations in a kind of "representative learning design" (Pinder, Davids,

Renshaw and Araújo, 2011) but initially in only one tactical situation (Memmert, 2004; Memmert and Harvey, 2010) with an innumerable variety of creative solutions (variability; see Chapter 4). Therefore, 1-**D**imension Games are, after **D**eliberate Play (see last section in this chapter), the next step in the continuum developed by Côté et al. (2007) and they may be categorised as structured practice. Psychological learning theories (cf. Chapter 4) show that children learn to transfer convergent and divergent tactical thinking to other team and racket sports. This means that tactical transfer of learning is feasible. For repetition, codes of acting are movements that are intrinsically tied to the targets. This means that the cognitive system does not control motion; rather, it controls action (Prinz, 1997). In specific situations, different attributes exist that exactly represent a specific structured situation. An example of those attributes may be structured conditions in team sport situations. For instance, two defenders have to be beaten in order for a pass to be played to one of a player's teammates. Accordingly, the aim of the action will be to use existing, located and originated gaps for passing. Subsequently, a movement will be selected and the action target or task solved appropriately.

1-Dimension games in team and racket sports

The application of 1-**D**imension Games for advancing creativity will now be described in more detail in the context of team and racket sports. 1-**D**imension Games can train elementary basic tactics, which are important in many different team and racket sports. Several denominations of tactical components across sport games exist, which do not differ significantly in content (cf. Griffin et al., 1997; Memmert and Harvey, 2010; Roth and Kröger, 2011). For example, the basic tactics by Memmert (2004) describe the fundaments of different team and racket sports (see Table 5.1). They were developed and validated in multiple single experiments, a longitudinal field-study and a transfer study (see Memmert, 2004; Memmert and Harvey, 2010).

1-**D**imension Games can help train one of the basic tactical components in isolation (for example, "Identification of Gaps" from Table 5.1).

Example of a 1-Dimension game using the basic tactic "Identification of Gaps":

Two teams with five players each act towards two goals against each other (see Figure 6.6 a and Figures 7.1 a and b). The field is separated into two halves. In each half, three players play against two. The particular players cannot leave their field, and the outnumbered situation always takes place in front of their own goal. The aim of the attacking team is to shoot goals by recognising gaps in the opponent team, while the defending team tries to conquer the ball, recognise gaps between the players of the opponent team, and pass across the centre line towards their own attackers.

Table 5.1 Basic tactics across team and racket sports from Memmert (2004; see also Memmert and Harvey, 2010)

Attacking the goal: "Attacking the goal" includes the tactical requirement to make spatial and temporal decisions while solving tactical tasks or match situations by running towards the goal in order to execute the finishing action.

Taking ball near goal: "Taking ball near goal" includes the tactical requirement to transport the ball, together with team mates, to a finishing space.

Playing together: "Playing together" includes the tactical requirement to pass the ball to the partners quickly and in a manner suitable to the situation.

Using gaps: "Using gaps" includes the tactical requirement to make spatial decisions while solving tactical tasks or match situations by using gaps effectively.

Feinting: "Feinting" includes the tactical requirement of securing possession of the ball when dealing with opponents individually.

Achieving an advantage through supporting, orienting and cooperating with partners. "Achieving an advantage through supporting, orienting and cooperating with partners" includes the tactical requirement to achieve and create advantageous spaces by supporting and orientating to "get open" to receive a pass.

1-Dimension games in youth football

A prime example of the application of 1-**D**imension Games for the advancement of creativity is again within the context of football. Group tactical abilities in football are used as the content. In modern football, tactical skills play an important role in all age groups and at all proficiency levels (Memmert and Harvey, 2010; Memmert and König, 2007). Many experts regard tactics as the factor which gets the least attention in the training process (Greco, et al. 2010; Memmert and Roth, 2007). While there are a couple of journal articles in the area of group tactics, a systematic overview is not yet available. It is even more significant that there are no empirically validated differentiations of group tactical requirements in football. More specifically, taxonomies of group tactics occur sporadically in books, but it has not yet been shown whether these tactics are actually relevant in either amateur or competitive football. Therefore, Memmert (2006d) addressed those deficits in order to provide a scientifically-based analysis of football-specific group tactics (cf. Figure 5.3).

Altogether, 585 match situations were judged and commented on by coaches. During the recorded games, the trainers selected important positive and negative behaviours of different position groups without being aware of the fact that their coaching skills were being evaluated. The implicit expert knowledge (video sequences and comments) from the single case analysis was solidified with the help of further qualitative content analyses. The resulting offensive and defensive group tactical skills were allocated to superordinate basic categories by means of inductive categorisation. Thus, group tactical challenges were identified (see Table 5.2) that had to be solved through the cooperation of several team members

Table 5.2 List of six defensive and six offensive group tactics that result from inductive category formation and further qualitative evaluation steps (from Memmert et al., 2011)

Defense	
Quick regrouping	• Group tactical requirement, which demands that position groups prevent their opponent's attacks through quick changes from offense to defense
Pressing	• Group tactical requirement, which demands that position groups disturb the offense actions of their opponent as early as possible
Man to man marking	• Group tactical requirement, which demands that the members of a position groups are aware of the marking of their opponents e.g. during corner kicks or man-marking in general
Competing for the second ball	• Group tactical requirement, which demands that position groups and individual players position themselves adequately in order to win second balls (e.g. after goal-kicks or tacklings)
Communication	• Group tactical requirement, which demands that position groups keep their orientation on the pitch by making adequate use of previously agreed codewords
Support play	• Group tactical requirement, which demands that position groups gain ball possession or avoid shots on goal by an appropriate position play

Offense	
Attacking play	• Group tactical requirement, which demands that position groups initiate play by systematic actions, e.g. vertical passes
Combination play	• Group tactical requirement, which demands that position groups keep the ball possession through double passes, short passes or triangular passes
Switch play	• Group tactical requirement, which demands that position groups create space by passing the ball from one side of the pitch to the other
Creating space	• Group tactical requirement, which demands that position groups choose adequate paths (e.g. cross-over and dummy runs in order to give each other space
Wing play	• Group tactical requirement, which demands that position groups pose a goal threat on the wings e.g. by through-balls
Counter attacks	• Group tactical requirement, which demands that position groups try to intersect the defense quickly, e.g. by playing through balls
Set pieces	• Group tactical requirement, which demands that position groups create a goal threat through free kicks, corner kicks and throw-ins.
Setting up shots on goal	• Group tactical requirement, which demands that position groups try to pass to their team mates so that they can score a goal from a long or short distance

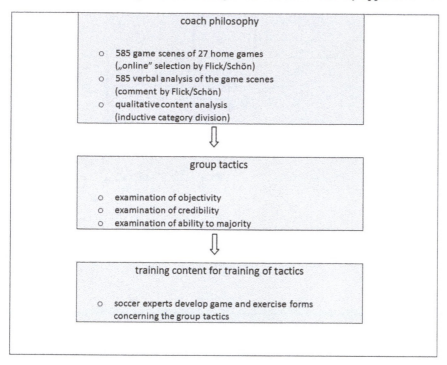

Figure 5.3 Design of the research methodological procedure

(position groups). Such position groups were, for instance, strikers or midfielders, but could also be players in certain areas (e.g. left and right wing) or players from different positions that move across those areas at a particular moment.

The methodological realisation of the six defensive and offensive football-specific components can occur in 1-Dimension Games. As an example, the group tactical content "pressing" is trained in the following game (cf. Figure 5.4). Four defence players plus the goalkeeper compete against four attacking players (1:4:4). The game opening is made by the goalkeeper. The attacking players leave the left or right defence player free on purpose and double him immediately after the lead. The other players engage. The offence tries to achieve a successful and fast goal completion after stealing the ball. After the game interruption, the game is continued by the goalkeeper. The aim of the defence players is that one player dribbles across the centre line.

The game takes place on one half of the actual field with a big goal. The following rules are in place:

- A return pass is not permitted!
- The offence can also act when outnumbered.
- Offsides are allowed to be played.
- The initial position can vary.

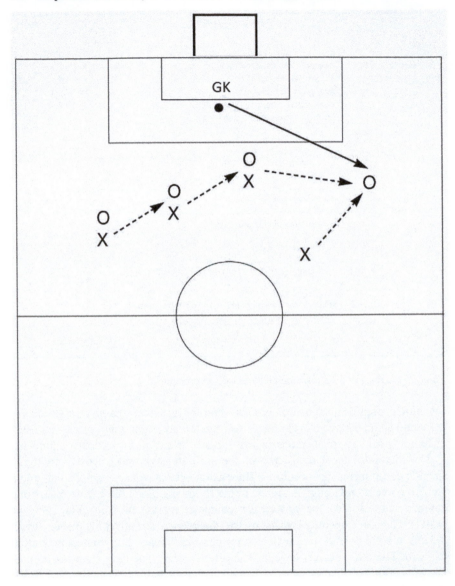

Figure 5.4 Representation of the game form "pressing"

Tactical creativity and diversification

The culture of playing in the streets and in parks has nowadays mostly disappeared
in our society. New buildings take away potential playing areas in cities and
strongly restrict the possibilities for the development of our children. In previous
generations children grew up playing in the streets, in parks or in courtyards, and

therefore they learned to play with different kinds of balls. They also profited from the varied experience and perception of situations in team and racket sports during childhood. "In our experience the best novice football players are those with experience of field hockey, ice hockey, basketball or other invasion games, because these players already understand the spatial aspects of football. Tactically these games are similar even though the skills used are completely different" (Griffin, Mitchell and Oslin, 1997, p. 9).

Not only did they learn various techniques like throwing, catching or kicking without guidance or instruction, but they also sorted constellations of teams and games (group size, rules, material of the ball) before they knew about certain tactical features. An extensive environment often leads to denser dendritic branching and a higher number of synapses (Menzel, 2001; see also Chapter 2). In addition, Ward, Finke and Smith (2002) showed that a combination of different, initially separately-stored concepts is jointly responsible for creative solutions. Furthermore, the effect of knowledge with different complexity or abstraction levels seems to play a crucial role in divergent thinking processes. The desired diversification can be achieved by the variable attempts at and discovery of solutions with different motoric embodiments (hand, foot and implements). Thus, games can be performed by foot or hand, as well as with a hockey-stick; the goal of the game stays the same.

Due to many different experiences of movement with the application of different motor skills, more precise relations can be built. An adaption to prospectively learned experiences of movement is easier to recognise for the learner because he can resort to a potential of relations (Memmert, 2011; Schöllhorn et al., 2006).

Involvement in a diverse range of sports and physical activities may be valuable for the development of creativity. Current theoretical approaches (e.g. Sternberg and Lubart, 1995) support the view that gathering diversified experiences over a number of years is ideal for the development of creativity. Diversification is supported by theoretical models (Simonton, 1999; Sternberg, 1999) and empirical evidence from research on creativity-related context variables (Csikzentmihalyi, 1999; Martindale, 1990; Simonton, 1996).

Results of studies on eminent athletes' reports have also suggested that gathering game experience in a number of different games is an ideal medium for sport players' creative development (Hamsen, Greco and Samulski, 2000). Further, recent research suggests that some sports participation in other activities could play a functional role in the development of expertise (Baker, 2003). The players still benefit from the varied perceptions of situations in sport games gathered during their childhood (Baker, Côté and Abernethy, 2003). Baker et al. (2013) found that an early breadth of exposure to other sports correlates inversely with the amount of sport-specific training that is necessary to maintain expert-level proficiency in basketball, netball and field hockey. The authors assumed that the acquisition of skills necessary for high-level performance is easier when an early involvement in other sports takes place. For general cognitive skills such as pattern recognition, a transferability across domains exists where offensive and defensive structures are similar (Abernethy, Baker and Côté, 2005).

In a longitudinal research programme it was shown that the perception of and experience in many different sport game situations has a positive influence on the development of tactical creativity (Memmert and Roth, 2007). The efficacy of various training approaches in team and racket sports for the development of tactical creativity was investigated. A group of 135 children aged around seven years took part in a fifteen-month field-based study in which they participated either in non-specific treatment groups, a specific handball, football or field hockey group, or a control group. General and game-oriented tactical creativity as dependent variables were measured with game-test-situations (cf. Memmert, 2007, and Chapter 7). The analysis of treatment-related effects showed that the areas in which the groups were trained (i.e. football, handball, hockey) were precisely the areas in which they showed significant improvements. This could be interpreted as evidence for specific training effects (**D**eliberate Practice, see this Chapter); however, this interpretation must be considered relative to evidence of clear transfer effects regarding tactical creativity in team and racket sports. Non-specific experiences (**D**eliberate Play, see this Chapter) seem to be a promising alternative to specific treatments (see Figure 5.5). Unlike motor competencies, it seems possible to train tactical creativity independently from movement techniques. Finally, the authors conclude "that non-specific and specific concepts are on a more or less similar level in terms of creativity development. As the comparisons of the percentage increase in the treatment phases have shown, the non-specific approaches can even prove to be more effective in the long term" (p. 1429).

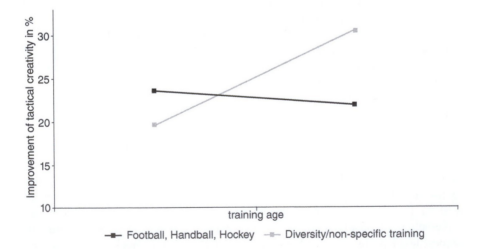

Figure 5.5 Development (in %) of the improvement of tactical creativity as a function of training age and training content

Tactical creativity and deliberate coaching

Haven't we all seen situations where children play while not noticing a completely freestanding teammate and therefore don't include him in the play? Occasionally, teammates or coaches accuse the player in possession of the ball of not having seen a completely freestanding player and not passing the ball towards him, even though he was located directly in the alleged focus of attention. The accused player then rejects all accusations and affirms that he just did not see the better positioned player directly in front of him.

An explanation for this example can be the phenomenon of inattentional blindness (Mack and Rock, 1998; Most et al., 2005). The failure to detect an unexpected object if attention is diverted to another task or object is called "inattentional blindness". Only when attention is focused on a certain area information is consciously absorbed and processed. When attention is assigned to a different object, an unexpected object is often not perceived, even though it is located in the field of vision of the person. Inattentional blindness can be credited as an essential factor within the limited information processing capacity of human beings.

Two examples are offered to clarify the phenomenon of inattentional blindness:

In a (unfortunately) true occurence (Chabris, Weinberger, Fontaine and Simons, 2011) a policeman pursued a thief on foot through a deserted industrial area. While doing so, he ran directly past a fight in which two men were beating up another man. The policeman did not stop to intervene. Later he said in court that he did not notice the fight (with fatal consequences).

A cyclist was talking on his mobile phone while cycling through a city. Suddenly a big dog appeared and ran across the street. The dog was hit by the bike and the cyclist fell down. Later, the fortunately not seriously injured cyclist affirmed that he did not notice the dog consciously, even though it was standing directly in front of him on the pavement for some time.

Inattentional blindness has become a well-established concept among other dimensions of attention (e.g. "sustain attention", "focus attention") in the field of psychology (see Most et al., 2005 for a review), and now it has also been investigated in complex daily situations (i.e. phone calls while driving a car: Strayer, Drews and Johnston, 2003; flight controllers: Cumming and Tsonis, 2005). Most impressive was the presentation of the inattentional blindness paradigm by Simons and Chabris (1999; see Figure 5.6).

These authors showed a twenty-three-second video to their participants, in which six people were passing two basketballs among each other. Subjects were given the task of counting the number of passes made between three basketball players. What was surprising about this experiment was that some subjects did not

Figure 5.6 Single frame with the unexpected gorilla from the famous basketball video by Simons and Chabris (1999). Figure provided by Daniel Simons, www.theinvisiblegorilla.com

notice that a gorilla was moving through the group as the game was played. In an experiment by Memmert, Simons, and Grimme (2006) it was demonstrated that there is no significant correlation between the conscious perception of unexpected objects (an inattentional blindness task; Simons and Chabris, 1999) and performance in the detection of peripheral stimuli (functional field of view task; Green and Bavelier, 2003) or attention distribution tasks (multiple-object tracking task; Alvarez & Franconeri, 2005).

As described above, tactical creativity is always associated with the ability to generate new and unusual solutions. For this reason, the inattentional blindness paradigm is well suited for research on creative processes, since attention performance is associated with the discovery of unexpected objects. In further studies (Memmert, 2006c), it was shown that inattentional blindness is not a perceptual constant and that it can be modulated by experiences (see also Drew, Võ and Wolfe, 2013). Conversely, age effects could occur, which is important for the development of specific training programmes (Memmert, 2006c). A further group of 112 subjects watched the above-described "basketball video" by Simons and Chabris (1999). Here they had to count the passes by the white players (the primary task). The results indicated significant differences between experts in basketball and non-experts in basketball. Skilled players consciously perceived the unexpected object with a likelihood of about 60%. Independent of expertise, age effects existed between children (aged eight years) and juniors/adults, but not between players aged fourteen and twenty-two years. For children, the likelihood of noticing the gorilla decreases to less than 10%.

Another study by Memmert (2010b) establishes a direct link between inattentional blindness, expertise and creativity. In this experiment, 116 trained and untrained children and adolescents from different age groups performed four standardised tasks in a cross-sectional design. They completed a general and a sport-specific inattentional blindness task, the computer-controlled inattentional blindness task devised by Most et al. (2005), and the handball-specific inattentional blindness test by Memmert and Furley (2007). In addition, they were provided with a general and a sport-specific creativity test. These tests were a subtest of the creativity test for pre-school and school children (KVS-P, Krampen, 1996) as a facet of divergent thinking, and a handball-specific creativity test based on Johnson and Raab (2003). The results show that the trained adolescents with the ability to notice the free player could also describe more original solutions in the handball-specific situation than the thirtten-year-olds, who were "blind" to the free team mate (see Figure 5.7 right). At this point, it should be mentioned that the effect reported for sports was also found across other domains. The untrained adolescents who achieved better performances in the general inattentional blindness task also fared better in the general creativity test in comparison to the participants who could not describe the unexpected object (see Figure 5.7 left; for more details, see Memmert, 2009a).

Following the inattentional blindness paradigm developed by Mack and Rock (1998) and Most et al. (2005), we conducted a series of further pre-experiments on attention with the aim of analysing the influence of special kinds of instruction on

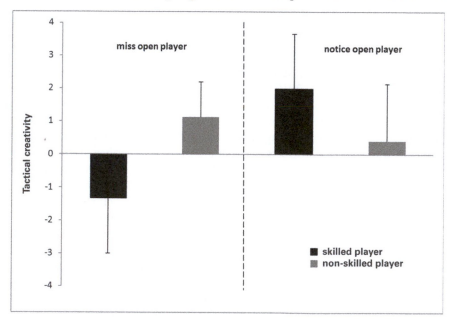

Figure 5.7 Tactical creativity scores (±SE) as a function of attention and expertise (data from Memmert, 2010b)

tactical decision making in team ball sports (Memmert and Furley, 2007; Furley, Memmert and Heller, 2010). We hypothesised that players do not find the best tactical solution even if they only receive a few further instructions, because of their reduced attention focus. More complex and sport-like problems were constructed for a series of experiments that built on each other.

In the first experiment by Memmert and Furley (2007; see Figure 5.8a), fourteen-year old juniors were instructed to focus their attention on their direct opponent (with the primary task of naming the position of their opponent at the end of the trial) in a handball-specific tactical decision making test. Participants were also required to simultaneously make a tactical decision (find a totally open player) that would most likely lead to a goal (the secondary task). 45% of the adolescents failed to notice the open team member. This result was replicated in basketball-specific situations with adults (Furley et al., 2010; see Figure 5.8b). Completely open team members were missed by approximately 40% of male basketball players. This effect was unchanged even in more realistic contexts with motor responses, as well as in a primary task closer to the field (triple selection task) (studies 2 and 3 in Furley et al. 2010).

In another experiment by Memmert and Furley (2007), participants were confronted with exactly the same tasks. However, one group received more tactical instructions than the other group (narrow/broad breadth of attention) in order to investigate the influence of these instructions on the tactical decision. The results indicated that more specific instructions prior to the tactical decision led to inferior tactical decisions compared to fewer instructions. In the critical video trial in the last experiment by Memmert and Furley (2007), the open team member was waving his hands in order to signal that he was unmarked. Only one participant failed to notice the open team member here.

A further field-based study on training units dealt with the question of whether the results obtained in the studies on tactical decision making (Memmert and Furley, 2007; Furley et al., 2010) could be directly translated into practical training concepts. Here, I introduce the term "breadth of attention", which refers to the number and range of stimuli that a subject attends to at any time. The simplest way to change the breadth of attention is to influence the individual's scope of attention with different instructions from a coach. As described above, current models of attention and perception show that human beings can only see certain things actively and explicitly, specifically which they want to perceive or which are absorbed by their attention – for example, through instructions (Most et al., 2005). A six-month longitudinal study examined different kinds of instructions by coaches during training sessions on the development of tactical creativity in the area of team sports (Memmert, 2007). Creative performance was measured by a real-world sport-specific creativity task (game test situation, see Chapter 6). A comparison between a control group and a treatment group that focused on training a narrow breadth of attention showed that the creative performance of the attention-broadening training group improved significantly (cf. Fig. 5.9).

In the attention-broadening training group, the teachers only defined the idea and the rules of the games, and no special tactical advice or any kind of feedback

Figure 5.8 Two sport-specific inattentional blindness test scenarios with different degrees of complexity (Above: little complexity, handball, 4 versus 4, Memmert & Furley, 2007; Below: middle complexity, basketball, 5 versus 5, Furley et al., 2010). Each of the freestanding team-players is encircled, and they – according expert opinion – are also the best option to play a pass to in this situation

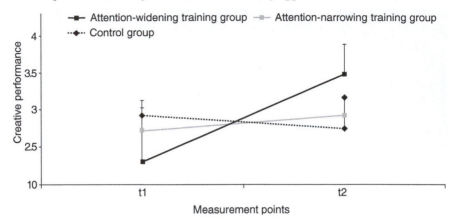

Figure 5.9 Development of tactical creativity as a function of attention training

regarding attention focus was given. As a result, the children learned to have a wide breadth of attention in complex situations (Memmert, 2007; see Figure 5.10a). The children in the attention-narrowing training group performed the same kind of exercises as the participants in the attention-broadening training group. The only difference concerned the role of the teachers. The coaches now gave the children certain, explicit tactical instructions and corrections for each game type. As such, only the trainers' instruction guidelines varied between the two training models. In contrast to the teaching models of the attention-broadening programme, this training programme (Teaching Games for Understanding; Griffin et al., 1997) discouraged the children from learning to direct their attention towards different kinds of stimuli. As a result of this narrow breadth of attention, not all stimuli and information that could lead to original and possibly unique solutions in a certain situation could be processed and associated with one another. The children learned to have a narrow breadth of attention in complex situations (see Figure 5.10b).

The focus on a wide breadth of attention requires the biggest modification of the Teaching Games for Understanding model when it is extended to younger children. In the Teaching Games for Understanding approach, the questions asked by coaches and teachers focus attention directly on different areas of the game, but the aforementioned studies suggest that less attention-guided instruction leads to a wider breadth of attention in children aged six to eight years. A wide breadth of attention makes it possible to associate different stimuli that may initially appear to be irrelevant. Hence, younger children would benefit from coaches lining up forms of play and practice and not posing any specific questions to the children during or after each game. Of course, older children should get specific instructions to learn specific if-then rules in particular sport settings.

A follow-up study with gifted children (IQ>130) showed the importance of attention performance and inattentional blindness for the development of tactical creativity (Memmert, 2006a). An initial experiment selected the inattentional blindness paradigm as an appropriate method to study individual differences in

Figure 5.10 By altering the instructions of the coaches or teachers it is possible to change the breadth of attention among children in 1-**D**imension Games. Fewer instructions lead to a wide breadth of attention (a), many instructions lead to a narrow breadth of attention (b)

the visual attention of gifted and non-gifted children. The results of the monitor task developed by Most et al. (2005) revealed significant differences between both samples. This can be interpreted as one reason why, in contrast to a gifted control group (gifted children without treatment) and a non-gifted treatment group, the creative performance of the gifted children significantly improved after a six-month training programme of creativity.

Overall, these findings stress the importance of focusing our attention on the training of creativity. A wide breadth of attention makes it possible to associate different stimuli that may initially appear to be irrelevant. Through deliberate and self-controlled play in complex situations, children should improve their divergent thinking. Hence, the aim of the training should be that the trainer gives reduced instructions to the children, parallel to his own standard solutions, and thus offers them the possibility to seek out and perceive unexpected and possibly better alternative solutions. This view stands in contrast to recent coaching behaviour in youth football. Partington, Cushion and Harvey (2014) revealed that the coaches of younger age football groups currently give more instruction than coaches of older age groups.

To be more concrete, the training experiment presented in this chapter encourages the view that less instruction by the coaches during game play leads to a wide breadth of attention and therefore facilitates greater improvements in tactical creativity. These findings support previous research on attention-narrowing environmental stimulations (Kasof, 1997), which found that people were not able to take in and associate all the stimuli and information that could lead to original and possibly unique solutions in a certain situation with a narrow breadth of attention. Moreover, a wide breadth of attention makes it possible to associate different stimuli that may initially appear to be irrelevant.

The findings reported above make it clear that teaching programmes for younger children should put special emphasis on giving fewer instructions to children. This means that forms of play must be chosen from the Teaching Games for Understanding approach in which the games are constructed in such a way that the "situations speak to the children". The teachers only give the idea and the rules of the games, nothing more (i.e. no special tactical advice or any kind of feedback). This view is supported by feedback research in the area of motor learning and recently in perceptual-cognitive learning. Memmert et al. (2009) showed that a lower frequency of feedback has no effect on perceptual learning performance in badminton, when compared to 100% feedback.

Hence, the aim of the training for children between six and eight should be that the trainer gives the children fewer instructions, parallel to his/her own standard solutions, and thus offers children the possibility to seek out and perceive unexpected and possibly better alternative solutions. In this way, discovery learning (cf. Bakker, Whiting and van der Burg, 1990), self-controlled learning (cf. Wulf and Toole, 1999) and engaged learning (cf. Renzulli, 1994) are feasible. One possible explanation for the aforementioned learning paradigms could be that actively involving learners in the learning process permits more effective information processing (cf. McNevin, Wulf, & Carlson, 2000). Moreover, greater emphasis is placed on implicit learning processes whose positive effects have long been discussed in the fields of psychology (cf. Reber, 1993), motor function research (cf. Magill, 1998), and sports science (cf. Farrow and Abernethy, 2002; see also Chapter 4).

Tactical creativity and deliberate motivation

As the model of Sternberg and Lubart (1991) describes, motivation is one factor that can influence creativity. It is well documented that individuals can learn and achieve better performances if they are having fun while performing a task (Amabile, 1996; Sternberg, 1988). In particular, being able to complete tasks without instruction, correction, restriction or teaching per se results in a way of learning that is effortless and enjoyable. The reason is that intrinsic motivation is promoted in the subject (Ryan and Deci 2000; Vallerand, 2001).

Numerous experiments from psychology provide compelling evidence that a "happy mood" (e.g. positive affect) can inspire creative performances (for an overview, see Isen, 2000), stimulate the production of innovative ideas (Isen, Daubman, & Nowicki, 1987) and stimulate the generation of unusual free associations (Hirt, Levine, McDonald, Melton and Martin, 1997). Beyond this, Friedman and Förster have presented further research that highlights the influence of attitude on the achievement of success in creative performances (cf. Friedman and Förster, 2000, 2001).

These results are currently associated with different motivationally-oriented theoretical models from social psychology (e.g. Regulatory Focus Theory, Higgins, 1997; Theory of Personality Systems Interactions, Kuhl, 2000), which indicate that more than merely creative performance can be directly influenced by the simplest of instructions, such as the emotional manipulation of participants. Higgins (1997) proposed two modes of self-regulation in order to regulate pleasure and suffering (i.e. to direct behaviour towards promotion or prevention targets). In one mode, a focus on accomplishments and aspirations was labeled as a promotion focus, and in the other mode the focus on safety and responsibilities was called a prevention focus (cf. Figure 5.11). More concretely, a promotion focus accounts for regulating pleasure as a positive result of action and suffering as an absence of positive results. A prevention focus, in contrast, refers to pleasure in the absence or successful avoidance of negative events, and suffering as when the negative events occur.

The regulatory systems of both promotion and prevention focus, with their different objectives, control the action of a person: the promotion focus system fulfills the need for care by constituting the approach of the ideal self as the desirable finite state. The ideal self conjoins hope, wishes, aspirations, and attempts. The prevention focus system, in contrast, regulates behaviour in relation to the target self through the representation of duties, responsibilities, and necessities. The needs for safety are fulfilled by this system.

Surprisingly, it is relatively easy to influence people towards one of the foci, e.g. by instruction. For instance, different labyrinths (the manipulation condition) are normally shown to subjects by psychologists before a creativity test (see

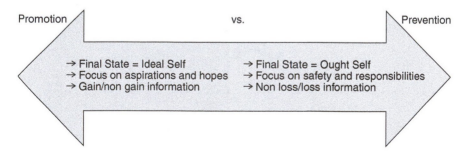

Figure 5.11 Theoretical framework by Higgins (1997). Personality can have specific shaping in regard to different strategies of achieving objectives. Two types of self-regulation are proposed in aiming for the desired target states in terms of a continuum of prevention and promotion

Figure 5.12a). In both conditions, the participants' task is to find a way for the mouse to get out of the maze. In the promotion-cue condition, a piece of cheese was depicted as lying outside the maze (instruction: "Show the mouse the way to the cheese!"). In the prevention-cue condition, instead of the cheese, an owl was depicted hovering above the maze (instruction: "How can the mouse escape from the owl?"). For better divergent performance it is sufficient for promotion instructions to be given to the participants. For example, during the handling of established creativity tests they have to push their hand from below against the counter top (arm flexion as promotion action) instead of pushing from above to the table (arm extension as prevention action; Friedmann and Förster, 2000).

In the sport context, a recent study by Memmert, Hüttermann and Orliczek (2013) was the first to show that divergent decision performance in sport benefits from promotion focus. In this experimental study, thirty football players had to name, under standardised conditions, as many decision options as possible when watching twenty football videos (Figure 5.12b). Parallel to the work of Friedmann and Förster (2001), identical labyrinths with different framings had previously been shown to them (cf. Figure 5.12a); half of the players had to find the way out so that the mouse reaches the cheese (promotion focus) while the other half had to resolve the labyrinth so that the mouse would not be caught by the owl (prevention focus). Foootball players generated more original and flexible solutions in the promotion than in the prevention condition (see Figure 5.13). However, these initial results must be confirmed and further scrutinised.

In addition to the framing possibility of a promotion or prevention focus, the personality or basic motivation of people tends to be more biased towards either promotion or prevention. Usually, the dispositional focus of a person can be easily evaluated using regulatory focus questionnaires (cf. Higgins et al., 2001; Summerville and Roese, 2008; Lockwood, Jordan and Kunda, 2002). Taking the

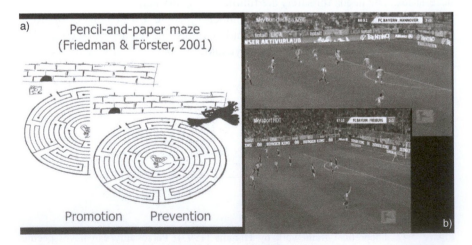

Figure 5.12 a) Stimuli material for promotion and prevention manipulation (with permission from Jens Förster); and b) two slides for the stimuli material of the sport-specific divergent thinking task (with permission from SKY, www.sky.de)

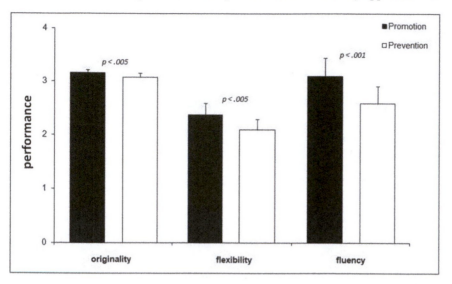

Figure 5.13 Representation of the three components of creativity: originality, flexibility and liquidity as a function of the manipulation of promotion vs. prevention

regulatory focus questionnaires by Lockwood et al. (2002) as an example, the participants or players have to answer eight promotion and nine prevention questions. All items are rated on a seven-point scale with endpoints labeled 1 ("not at all true of me") and 7 ("very true of me").

Examples of a promotion and prevention question of the modified (for the context of sport) regulatory focus questionnaires by Lockwood et al. (2002):

"I often worry that I will fail to accomplish my sporting goals." (prevention item)

"I often think about how I will achieve sporting success." (promotion item)

For example, Memmert and Cañal-Bruland (2009) showed that promotion-oriented participants, classified using the regulatory focus questionnaires of Lockwood et al. (2002), display faster reaction times in a selective attention task (cueing paradigm by Posner, 1980) than prevention-oriented participants. In a sport context, a study by Plessner, Unkelbach, Memmert, Baltes, and Kolb (2009) revealed systematic differences in chronic regulative orientation among athletes from different sports (cf. Figure 5.14), as measured by the regulatory focus questionnaires of Lockwood et al. (2002). The first goal was to show that sports with a clear aim to score goals, a high complexity in decision-making, and a great

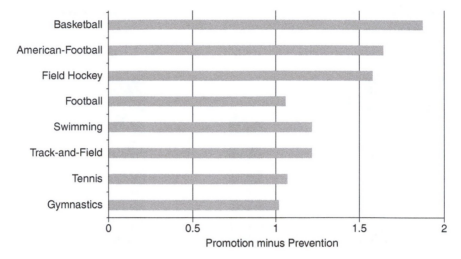

Figure 5.14 Means of the promotion and prevention values as a function of sport

variability in skill execution require athletes with a higher promotion orientation. Indeed, football and basketball players were found to be more promotion orientated, whereas gymnastics and track-and-field athletes as well as swimmers are more prevention orientated (cf. Figure 5.14). The latter highly-skilled sport activities contain situations that are less complex and the skill execution has to be much more stabilised. Therefore, it is the duty of the athletes such as swimmers to perform their tasks as accurately as possible.

The second goal of this study was to show that attackers are more focused on the ideal (scoring), whereas the tasks of defenders are usually more focused on the target (prevention of scoring). The fit of chronic dispositional orientation and task demand is not random in this case. For instance, attacking players in different sports are, on average, more promotion focused than defenders.

A further extension of the approach of Higgins (1997) is his regulatory fit theory (Higgins, 2000): the performance on a given task may depend on the fit between people's regulatory focus (promotion or prevention) and people's chronic regulatory orientation (promotion or prevention). This idea of better performance and a more positive effect via regulatory fit has already received some empirical support in the domain of cognitive tasks (e.g. Grimm, Markman, Maddox and Baldwin, 2008; Keller and Bless, 2006; Maddox, Baldwin and Markman, 2006; Shah, Higgins and Friedman, 1998).

For example, the participants in the study by Memmert, Unkelbach, and Ganns (2010) were influenced in regard to their motivational orientation before solving the inattentional blindness task by Simons and Chabris (1999; see Figure 5.6). This regulatory focus condition was produced by giving the participants the pencil-and-paper maze used by Friedman and Förster (2001), shown in Figure 5.12 a. Finally, the participants' chronic regulatory orientation was assessed again by the regulatory focus questionnaires of Lockwood et al. (2002). We found that participants in the Fit condition outperformed the participants in the Non-Fit condition in their ability to notice the unexpected object.

In an experimental sport study by Plessner et al. (2009), twenty football players had to shoot five penalties in a row under standardized conditions. For half of them, the task was described in terms of promotion (instruction: "Your aspiration is to score at least three times"), and for the others the task was described in terms of prevention (instruction: "Your obligation is not to miss more than two times"). Finally, the dispositional focus of each player was measured using the modified German version of the regulatory focus questionnaire by Lockwood et al. (2002). A regression analysis of the data showed a significant interaction effect between instruction (promotion vs. prevention) and the chronic focus of the players (promotion vs. prevention). Hence, the "Regulatory Fit" had a positive effect on the players' hit rates. After that, Memmert, Plessner and Maßmann (2009) were able to replicate these results in basketball. Athletes achieved a higher score in a three points throw task under "Fit" than under "Non-Fit" conditions.

Finally, as well as task framing by instructions and individual orientation, the main characteristics of the task at hand could be more promotion or prevention orientated. In a consumer-orientated psychological study with female participants, it was shown that choosing a lipstick activated a promotion focus, whereas choosing a condom activated a prevention focus (Werth and Förster, 2007a). In a sports context, from the perspective of a striker the penalty situation should be more of a prevention situation (about 75% likelihood to score based on current football statistics; cf. Dohmen, 2008) and, from the perspective of a goalkeeper, more a promotion situation (about 25% likelihood to save the ball based current football statistics; cf. Dohmen, 2008). Empirical data from Memmert et al. (2009) indeed showed that sport tasks per se have a motivational character. In this study, sport students rated different tasks from several team and racket sports (basketball, football, handball, hockey, tennis) regarding the required regulatory focus (promotion/prevention). As expected, the results showed that some sport-specific tasks, such as the free throw in basketball, the penalty in football, the jump shot in handball from the nine-metres line, the penalty shot in hockey, or the second serve in tennis, rather request a prevention focus. However, three-point throws, free kicks, seven-metre shots, short corners and the first serve demand a more promotion focus.

Overall, the findings suggest the need to continue this line of research by trying to manipulate promotion focus in an attempt to improve divergent tactical thinking in sport specific settings. In future research the influence of communication (trainer announcements or commands) in association with regulatory focus and fit theory in sports performance may be picked out as a central theme. For some time psychological research activities have dealt with the effects of self-controlled learning conditions (for overviews, see Boekaerts, 1999; Straka, 2000). In the field of motor research, studies have analysed the influence of self-controlled activity on the acquisition of motor skills (cf. Chiviakowsky and Wulf, 2002). Previous investigations have consistently demonstrated the advantages of self-controlled motor learning, but only in retention tests (see Wulf and Toole, 1999).

It may be expected that athletes with a chronic promotion focus will obtain a greater fit if the given instructions ("task framing") are promotion orientated. For instance, if the training content of a 1-**D**imension Game is to pass through gaps, then the instruction should not be "It is your responsibility to..." but instead "Your hope is that..." or "Your aim is to..." or "My wish is that...". More specifically: "My wish is that every third ball is kicked through gaps," not: "I expect you to kick every third ball through gaps."

Finally, it should be noted that previous experiments have been based on internally valid instructions that are less related to practice and are less externally valid. Therefore, they appear less realistic in the real world of sport. Thus, it is necessary to find and validate instructions which can be provided to the athlete as an intervention in training and can be accepted by the athlete. The **D**eliberate Motivation principle in the TCA for developing tactical creativity is implicitly contained in the Teaching Games for Understanding approach. Since the emphasis is on playing, it is associated with a certain degree of informality. "Learning is more effective when children enjoy what they are doing" (cf. Renzulli and Reis, 2000, p. 380). However, future sports-related studies must show which mechanisms can help to optimise the motivational states of children to facilitate the generation of unique and original solutions. The results from social psychology appear to provide some indication that this is a worthwhile exercise, and that it is likely to add value.

Tactical creativity and deliberate practice

As mentioned above, Deliberate Practice offers a task-centred training programme based on instructions. There is a substantial amount of research showing that sport-specific experiences over a long time (the ten-year rule of Ericsson, Krampe and Tesch-Römer, 1993) are necessary for the attainment of expertise (e.g. Helsen, Starkes and Hodges, 1998; Kalinowski, 1985; Monsaas, 1985; but see also Hambrick and Meinz, 2011; Macnamara, Hambrick and Oswald, 2014). These researchers from the field of expertise have spent considerable effort examining the acquisition of expert decision-making and sport performance. According to the theory of Deliberate Practice (see Ericsson, Krampe and Tesch-Römer, 1993), expertise in a given domain is the result of extended engagement in high-quality training. The Ericsson et al. theory is based on the assumption that the most beneficial form of training for acquiring sport skill involves sport-specific activities that are highly relevant to specific sport performance improvement, effortful (either cognitively or physically), and executed for the purpose of improving current performance rather than for inherent enjoyment. Our own data suggest that, especially for top team players in the highest national leagues or even in the national team, the number of hours of training activities (**D**eliberate Practice) makes the difference between more creative and less creative team sport players (Memmert et al., 2010). National league players started their specific sport significantly later than players in the next highest level of competition. However, there are also differences between sports. For example, basketball is significantly different from other sports (e.g. football) in regard to the age at which training begins (about ten years), total years of involvement (about 40% less than other sports), total time spent in play-like activities (about 50–75% less than other sports), time spent in play-like activities prior to age fourteen (about 50–75% less than the other sports), and the number of other sports players were involved in (only about 2.5).

This evidence provides the basis for the convergence of two prevalent research paradigms, namely expertise research and creativity research, which have not yet been discussed in the same context (see Chapter 8). These two paradigms suggest that practice experiences (**Deliberate Practice**) and early play (**Deliberate Play**) have an important influence on the development of creativity in sports. In this case, specific experiences over a long time (ten or more years) are necessary for the development of expertise (e.g. Helsen, Starkes and Hodges, 1998). At the same time, current theoretical models regarding the development of creativity (Sternberg and Lubart, 1995) support the view that gathering diversified and even non-specific experiences (such as unstructured play) over time is an ideal medium for the development of creative thinking.

Deliberate Play and **Deliberate Practice** have direct parallels in the Teaching Games for Understanding approach. Deliberate playing is given top priority, as it is the central focus of the teaching invasion game approach (see also Play Practice, Launder, 2001; and the Tactical-Decision Learning Model, Grehaigne, Wallian and Godbout, 2005). Kidman and Lombardo (2010) noted: "The game is the teacher". In this way, all forms of play and practice that have been developed so far, accounting for age adaptations, can be applied to the development of creative behaviour in younger children. Through deliberate and self-controlled play in ecologically valid situations, the children should improve their tactical creativity.

Summary

The TCA, including the six **D**s for developing tactical creativity, has been described in more depth and with empirical support; all of them are useful concepts to enhance tactical creativity. In basic-element games, uninstructed and instructed play can lead to trying out a substantial amount of different tactical solutions (**Deliberate Play, Deliberate Practice**). Alongside small-sided games for the training of technical skills or fitness components of football players (Hill-Haas et al., 2011; Clemente et al., 2012), I introduce the term 1-**D**imension Games (structured games) for the development of non-specific and specific tactical competencies in team and racket sport. The idea is that a fixed number of players and defined rules and environmental constraints exist in basic tactical constellations, and the players are prompted to produce adequate and creative solutions. For **D**iversification, different motor skills in basic-element games can be used to support the development of creative solutions. The results of several presented studies made clear that simple instructions lead to a reduced attention focus, and the essential characteristics of a situation (e.g. open players) are not taken into account in decision making. For this reason, it is important – particularly in team and racket sports such as football, hockey, and basketball, in which the generation of tactical response patterns and original solutions are critical – that young players receive fewer instructions if the goal is to develop creativity, as this may increase their capacity to deal with unexpected situations (**Deliberate Coaching**). In addition, this chapter clarifies the existence of a close connection between motivation and creativity. Based on the regulatory focus theory, studies were described which showed that single motivational instructions can influence a number of cognitive and motor performance outcomes in a positive way. Particularly, promotion instructions motivate children to find creative and original solutions (**Deliberate Motivation**).

Empirical evidence suggests that all six of the **D**s can be useful methods to foster seldom and flexible solutions in team and racket sports. It should be the role of clubs and schools to try to create learning environments that allow the implementation of these methods. Therefore, structural and content changes may have to be made. For instance, sport specific training lessons (**Deliberate Practice**) could not be offered early on, perhaps offering the possibility of an unstructured form of **Deliberate Play** instead.

Discussion questions

1   What is the difference between small-sided games and 1-**D**imenson Games?
2   Do you think it is possible to create tactical transfer of theoretical deliberations and empirical results with 1-**D**imenson Games? See information from Chapter 4!
3   For the development of tactical creativity, why and how can you use **D**iversification?
4   Describe other concepts of motor learning (differential learning, variability of practice hypothesis) in the context of the methodical rule of **D**iversification. Link these concepts to a more tactical concept such as decision making.
5   For developing tactical creativity in young children, how can you use the concept of **D**eliberate Play?
6   Are there more examples for inattentional blindness that might have happened to you previously?
7   Try to explain the association between attention and tactical creativity on the basis of theoretical deliberations and experimental research.
8   Provide reasons for why coaches and/or teachers should maintain a low profile when using tactical instructions, and discuss what can occur when players direct excessive attention to individual aspects of the game.
9   What is a focus of prevention or promotion? Explain this on the basis of task constraints, instructions, and personality, and provide examples for team and racket sports.
10   Try to produce tactical instructions from different sports and phrase them in a way that a focus of prevention or promotion is evoked by the players.
11   For developing tactical creativity in young children, how could you use the concept of **D**eliberate Practice, and how does this concept become more and more important during adolescence?

Additional reading

Abernethy, B., Baker, J. & Côté, J. (2005) Transfer of pattern recall skills may contribute to the development of sport expertise. *Applied Cognitive Psychology*, 19, 705–718.

Baker, J., Côté, J. & Abernethy, B. (2003) Sport specific training, deliberate practice and the development of expertise in team ball sports. *Journal of Applied Sport Psychology*, 15, 12–25.

Ericsson, K.A., Krampe, R. & Tesch-Römer, C. (1993) The role of deliberate practice in the acquisition of expert performance. *Psychological Review*, 100, 363–406.

Greco, P., Memmert, D. & Morales, J.C.P. (2010) The effect of deliberate play on tactical performance in basketball. *Perceptual and Motor Skills*, 110, 849–856.

Higgins, E.T. (1997) Beyond pleasure and pain. *American Psychologist*, 52, 1280–1013.

Higgins, E.T. (2000) Making a good decision: Value from fit. *American Psychologist,* 55, 1217–1230.

Hill-Haas, S.V., Dawson, B., Impellizzeri, F.M. & Coutts, A.J. (2011) Physiology of small-sided games training in football: A systematic review. *Sports Medicine*, 41, 199–220.

Mack, A. & Rock, I. (1998) *Inattentional Blindness.* Cambridge: MIT Press.

Memmert, D. (2007) Can creativity be improved by an attention-broadening training program? An exploratory study focusing on team sports. *Creativity Research Journal*, 19, 1–12.

Memmert, D. & Furley, P. (2007) "I Spy With My Little Eye!": Breadth of attention, inattentional blindness, and tactical decision making in team sports. *Journal of Sport and Exercise Psychology*, 29, 365–347.

Memmert, D. & Roth, K. (2007) The effects of non-specific and specific concepts on tactical creativity in team ball sports. *Journal of Sport Science*, 25, 1423–1432.

Memmert, D., Baker, J. & Bertsch, C. (2010) Play and practice in the development of sport-specific creativity in team ball sports. *High Ability Studies*, 21, 3–18.

Memmert, D., Hüttermann, S. & Orliczek, J. (2013) Decide like Lionel Messi! The Impact of Regulatory Focus on Divergent Thinking in Sports. *Journal of Applied Social Psychology*, 43, 2163–2167.

Most, S.B., Scholl, B.J., Clifford, E.R. & Simons, D.J. (2005) What you see is what you set: Sustained inattentional blindness and the capture of awareness. *Psychological Review*, 112, 217–242.

Plessner, H., Unkelbach, C., Memmert, D., Baltes, A. & Kolb, A. (2009) Regulatory fit as a determinant of sport performance. *Psychology of Sport and Exercise*, 10, 108–115.

Schöllhorn, W., Michelbrink, M., Beckmann, H., Trockel, M., Sechelmann, M. & Davids, K. (2006). Does noise provide a basis for the unification of motor learning theories? *International Journal of Sport Psychology,* 37, 1–21.

6 How to measure tactical creativity in team and racket sports?

The question now arises of how the tactical creativity of individual players can be measured in team and racket sports. This is certainly more difficult and implies a bigger effort than simply clocking the hundred-metre time of a sprinter. However, there are objective and valid possibilities for measuring creativity, which we will describe in this chapter: game observation, video tests, and game test situations (cf. Memmert, 2013).

Three different characteristics are often utilised for the operationalisation of tactical creativity, namely originality, flexibility, and fluency, which Guilford (1967) identified by means of factor analysis.

- **Originality:** The exceptionality of tactical solutions can be rated by experts.
- **Flexibility:** The variety of tactical solutions is determined by the diversity of actions/answers from "test persons".
- **Fluency:** The number of tactical solutions people generate for a specific match situation.

For example, it is possible that a player exhibits a high number of adequate solutions, but all of them are based on pass feints (high fluency, low flexibility). Another player may point out only few solutions but include different feints such as body or shot feints (low fluency, high flexibility). Below, different test procedures for the evaluation of tactical creativity in team sports are presented. They can be classified along a continuum between ecological validity and artificial laboratory settings (cf. Figure 6.1).

The test procedures are depicted according to this criterion, and their specific advantages and disadvantages for a successful realisation of divergent tactical thinking performances will be discussed. Table 6.1 gives an overview of the specific possibilities and limitations of all three approaches (game observation, video tests and game test situations), which will be discussed in more depth in the next three sub-sections.

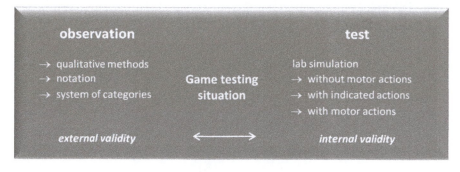

Figure 6.1 Systematisation of the procedures to diagnose tactical creativity (see Memmert and Roth, 2003)

Game observation

A central aspect of traditional game analysis is to quantify the complex qualitative information in a game such as football or basketball (Franks, 1985; Wright, Atkins, Bryan and Todd, 2013). Specifically for game playing ability (convergent tactical thinking), a number of assessment tools were developled which can discriminate between more and less advanced players (cf. Almond, 1986; French and Thomas, 1987; Turner and Martinek, 1992). Also, current technology provides a variety of measurement tools which can evaluate game performance (cf. Chen and Rovegno, 2000; Gréhaigne, Godbout and Bouthier, 1997; Nevett, Rovegno, Barbiaz and McCaughtry, 2001; Oslin, Mitchell and Griffin, 1998; Richard, Godbout and Gréhaigne, 2000; Richard, Godbout, Tousignand and Gréhaigne, 1999). These methods are constantly being improved (cf. Memmert & Harvey, 2008).

Decision making can be evaluated by using game play protocols (cf. French et al., 1996a, 1996b; French and Thomas, 1987; Jones and Farrow, 1999; McPherson and French, 1991; Turner, 1996; Turner and Martinek, 1992). For example, Gréhaigne et al. (1997) devised the Team Sport Assessment Procedure to measure game play performance in invasion games. This instrument takes the two basic notions of how a player gains possession of the ball and disposes of it into consideration. Oslin and colleagues (1998) developed a Game Performance Assessment Instrument to measure "game performance behaviors that demonstrate tactical understanding, as well as the player's ability to solve tactical problems by selecting and applying appropriate skills" (Oslin et al., 1998, p. 231).

The focus of such quantifications is the frequency and success of specific actions, such as passes or moves (cf. Figure 6.2). It is usually used to scout players or an entire team. Therefore, individual tactical components including pass success rate, pass direction, touches per individual ball possession, the number of long passes and crosses, number of misplaced long passes and the amount of dribbling can be evaluated. Additionally, group and team tactics, such as the number of passes during an attack, the number of passes in an attack leading to an attempt on target or a goal, the transition to defence after turnovers, the transition

Figure 6.2 Screenshot of a surface to analyse sequences of a football match (Mastercoach)

to offense after winning ball possession, and the type of playmaking, as well as actions in the opponent's penalty box, could be of importance.

Thus, it is now possible for experts in football to evaluate which actions are creative and which actions are not. More quantitatively, football experts or raters can also count how many times a player acted differently in a specific situation (fluency), how adequate and rare the player's solutions were (originality), and how many different kinds of solutions were generated for a specific situation (flexibility).

As shown in Figure 6.3, technological advancements allow the automatic recording of position data of players and the ball, enabling the reconstruction of tactical patterns (Baca, Dabnichki, Heller and Kornfeind, 2009). Furthermore, it is now possible to classify action processes in football by means of neural networks, and to check the identified process types with regard to their effectiveness.

Once position-oriented tactical patterns are recognised by means of a correspondingly trained neural network (cf. Chapter 2), it is simple to automatically count transitions between such patterns with respect to the corresponding actions. This leads to a matrix of transition probabilities, as shown in Figure 6.4. Moreover, if the corresponding trajectory network is calibrated to record the success of the represented process, a second matrix can be generated representing the success of those transitions. Using this approach, Memmert and Perl (2009b) rapidly demonstrated that out of 5,903 complex, real-life behaviours in team sports, only 1% of all tactical decisions were passes over the defenders to the opposite side (a lob shot).

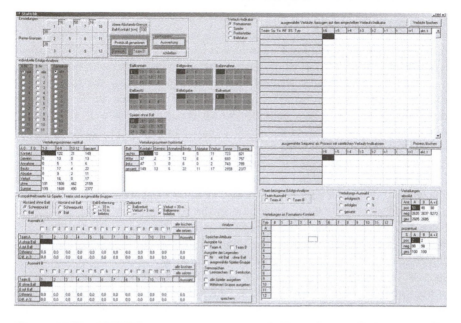

Figure 6.3 The SOCCER programme can automatically analyse tactical patterns of a match (Perl et al., 2013)

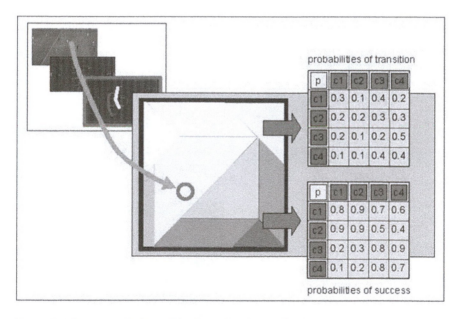

Figure 6.4 Process analysis resulting in statistical contributions

The probabilities of transitions and their success aid game analysis. The informational-theoretical relevance of actions can be estimated using their time-dependent frequency profiles. Under the assumption that a creative action is both rare and adequate, its information-theoretic relevance, together with the semantic evaluation of its adequacy, enables measuring and analysing the creativity of actions in an ecologically valid setting. In particular, activities can be recognised that indicate creativity (i.e. activities which are original as well as adequate solutions to the situation) (Grunz et al., 2012). An example of this recognisable creativity in football would be a rare combination of several difficult, direct passes or no-look passes which lead to a goal.

An advanced application of neural networks is the simulation of tactical behaviour, creative actions and dynamic learning in games. The action under assessment, such as a tactical decision in the game process or the movement behaviour of the athlete, is tested within the network and activates the corresponding neuron, which then returns information in different semantic categories, such as the type of activity, degree of creativity, probability of success, or probability of transition to other activities. The goal is to replace the current activity with a simulated one which could be more creative or more successful when activated in a game situation. More specifically, the resulting simulated process could improve the team's tactical behaviour. Mapped onto a network, this means that neurons should possess the ability to represent not only frequent but also rare actions. If such a net is calibrated with respect to success or adequacy, the time series of a process will be mapped to a trajectory, where the neurons can be programmed to correspond to creative actions. For example, new

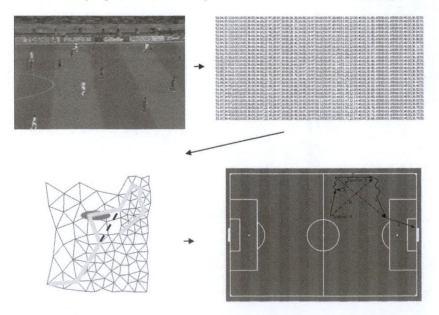

Figure 6.5 Illustration of the procedure of video data processing, including position data, neural networks, and the identification or simulation of creative plays in football

tactical actions of the athletes as specific tactical combinations over the wings in football could be developed theoretically or pragmatically and directly tested in a neural network simulation (cf. Figure 6.5).

Game test situations

Different types of instruments have been developed to evaluate an athlete's tactical decision-making skills. Currently, only a few sport-specific tactical creativity tasks have been constructed and tested for objectivity, reliability, and validity (Memmert et al., 2010). These include game test situations, which act as a type of compromise between standardised video tests and game observation methods.

Definition

Game Test Situations are the testing and diagnostic version of 1-Dimension Games. They contain contextual, real-world representations that provoke valid, creative solutions. In recurring, comparable situations, this competition setting evokes creative behaviour in specific 1-Dimension Games. Game idea, number of players, rules, and environmental conditions are given. The competition settings could involve different kinds of skills (hand, foot, or implement) in a system where the players take turns (two rounds for each person), thus meaning that positions and team players/opponents are systematically varied.

1-Dimension Games for the development of tactical creativity in game test situations are simple game forms with clearly defined game ideas, fixed numbers of players, defined rules, and consistent environmental conditions. The athlete's creative behaviour is assessed without standardising the ball's path and the actions of teammates and opponents. Hence, the fundamental idea consists of basic tactical constellations with clearly allocated roles in order to create recurring and consistent conditions with many repetitions for the participants (see 1-Dimension Games in team and racket sports and in football, Chapter 5).

Thus, game test situations (such as 1-Dimension Games) based on the methodological framework by Brunswik (1955) are termed *representative task design* (cf. Pinder et al., 2011). This approach emphasises the importance of studying organism-environment interactions which are seldom possible in laboratory settings. For example, Button, Dicks, Haines, Barker and Davids (2011) and Dicks, Button and Davids (2010) showed significant differences between video simulation conditions and in situ conditions with respect to information pickup for perception and action. Real-world tasks like 1-Dimension Games or game test situations offer a representative design to test tactical creativity in realistic, dynamic scenarios of team and racket sports.

Table 6.1 Advantages and disadvantages of different tests to measure tactical creativity: a detailed comparison between video tests, game test situations, and game observation (extension on the basis of Memmert, 2013)

	Video tests	*Game test situations*	*Game observation*
Complexity	Low	High	High
Confundations (team mate, etc.)	Low	Middle to high	High
Motor-action coupling	Only middle	High	High
Interaction	Low	Middle	High
Authenticity of situations	Low	middle	High
Transferability in practice	Low	High	High
One-dimensional structure of tasks	Given	Nearly given	Not given
Density of relevant actions	High	Middle to high	Middle to less
Relative consistency of conditions	High	middle	Less
Experimental manipulations	High	Middle to high	Zero

For example, in recurring, comparable situations, one game test situation evoked tactical behaviour in the identification of gaps (see Figure 6.6 a; see also Chapter 7, Figure 7.1). In this test situation, the attackers attempted to play the ball past the three defenders and below the upper boundary into the opposite field. Additionally, another task evoked tactical behaviour in off-the-ball movements (see Figure 6.6 b; see also Chapter 7, Figure 7.2). Here, the attackers had the task of passing the ball among themselves as often as possible without the defenders gaining possession of the ball. One variation of this task requires the test person to operate with different forms of motor actions, e.g. with hands, feet or hockey sticks (Memmert and Roth, 2007).

Performances in game test situations are always confounded by other performance aspects. For example, motor skills interact with tactical solutions. Of course, the technical skills of a player have an influence on the solution of tactical situations. The evaluation of technical skills must be avoided so that one does not unconsciously assess the observed motor performances of the test

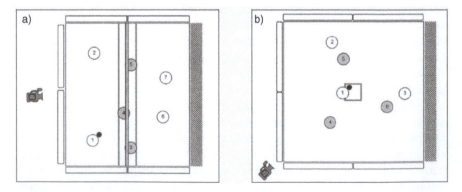

Figure 6.6 An overview of the GTS "Identification of gaps" and "Orienting and supporting"

person, but rather concentrates exclusively on the expected tactical actions of the player. In principle the observation of motor actions for the assessment of tactical actions is possible in videos too, but this is rarely used and applicable only to a certain extent. In game test situations, however, the motor-action coupling is inevitable.

In order to analyse creative actions, a video of the recorded behaviour is subsequently rated with regard to specific concepts by several independent experts. With the help of experts, application rules were developed and a scale was anchored. For example, Figure 6.7 illustrates the scaling for the GTS "Identification of gaps".

Originality of solutions to the situation (using gaps or passing)	Flexibility in the solutions to the situation (using gaps or passing)	Sca-ling	Anchor examples
Way above average (very unusual)	Two or more (different, original actions)	10	The subject demonstrated different highly unusual solutions to the situations. The gaps and passes found were absolutely unique.
Way above average (unusual)	Two or more (different, original actions)	9	The subject demonstrated different unusual solutions to the situations. Finding of gaps or passes was unique.
Above average (rare)	Two (different, original/rare actions)	8	The subject demonstrated different, still unusual solutions to the situations. The gaps and passes found were very rare.
Average (rather rare)	Two (different, rare actions)	7	The subject demonstrated two different solutions to the situations which were not unusual, but still very rare. The gaps and passes found were very surprising.
Average (quite rare)	Two (different, rare/new actions)	6	The subject demonstrated two different solutions to the situations, which were not unusual, but rare. The gaps and passes found were surprising.
Just below average (still new)	One (rare action)	5	The subject demonstrated one solution to the situations which wasn't the usual standard, but which had already occurred. The gaps and passes found were still innovative.
Just below average (very little new)	One (new action)	4	The subject demonstrated one solution to the situations which wasn't the usual standard, but which had already occurred often. The gaps and passes found were still innovative.
Below average (rather standard)	none	3	The subject generally offered standard solutions to the situations which had been displayed often. The gaps and passes found were rarely innovative.
Way below average (almost all standard)	none	2	The subject almost exclusively offered standard solutions to the situations which had all been displayed already. The gaps and passes found were very rarely innovative.
Way below average (only standard)	none	1	The subject only offered standard solutions to the situations. The gaps and passes found were never new.

Figure 6.7 Scaling for the evaluation of tactical creativity in the GTS "Identification of gaps" (Memmert and Roth, 2007)

In the assessment, a global estimation of overall game actions was made. First, the rater was required to rate each action made on a scale of 1 to 10. For better orientation, there is information given in the first two columns (aspect of quality and difficulty). The final evaluation result does not have to be an average value. Indications are the anchor examples in the last column. The definitions of attributes and scales have to be provided to the raters and have to be carefully discussed. All regulations and anchorages of the scales are explained in detail.

To evaluate usability, game test situations and concept-oriented expert ratings must be measured by quality criteria from classic testing theory. The main focus should be the determination of the inter-rater reliability of the rating procedure. "Rater reliability or objectivity is the degree to which the performance of a person is scored the same by two or more raters" (Safrit and Wood, 1989, p. 46). An important question in this respect is whether it is possible that the rating result is no longer dependent on the judgments of experts. Another important aspect of evaluation objectivity is intra-rater reliability. This evaluates how consistently the same observer gives the same performance score in repeated ratings of the same object. These aspects are considered simultaneously with the inter-rater reliability coefficient. By transformation of the inter-rater reliability coefficient, it is possible to calculate the degree of evaluation objectivity that a whole group of future raters will demonstrate in regard to specific attributes.

Standardized video tests

Tactical creativity video tasks are a highly standardised way of testing creativity (for current examples in the area of team and racket sports, see Johnson and Raab 2003; Memmert, 2010a, 2010b; Memmert et al., 2013).

Definition

In a standardised video test, participants watch sport-specific videos. The image is frozen after a certain time (e.g. one minute) has elapsed. The participants have to imagine themselves as the acting player and describe all the opportunities that might possibly lead to a goal. The answers are evaluated according to the criteria of originality, flexibility, and fluency.

Athletes view brief video sequences of a sports game (e.g. basketball, football) involving both attacking and defending players. At the end of the video clip, the final image is frozen with one player in possession of the ball. The participant takes over the role of the ball holder in the video clip and identifies all opportunities that might possibly lead to a goal/basket (cf. Figure 6.8). The motor executions (e.g. pass with the non-dominant hand/foot, indirect pass) should also be mentioned. The athlete's answers are noted on a specially designed sheet that contains all appropriate decisions. The same observation criteria of originality, flexibility, and fluency are used to evaluate the athlete's performance as they are employed in the usual divergent thinking tasks in psychology. The originality of the proposed solutions is then rated by experts. For flexibility, all possible tactical decisions in each situation are categorised into a number of different kinds of solution options (e.g. perform a one-on-one action, no-look-pass, and pass with a feint). The precise number of appropriate answers given by a subject for each video scene is thus used to measure fluency.

The video tests are less complex (e.g. in terms of stimuli, response options etc.) than the game test situations or the game observation approach. A distinct advantage of the video tests is the clear test situations presented in the video sequences, so that almost no confounding variables (e.g. physiological or technical factors) appear. At present, the interactivity with the medium of the screen is quite low for most of the published approaches; in contrast, the interaction between offensive and defensive players as well as team members is always present in game test situations. The game test situations have a high authenticity in regard to complex match situations, which is not the case for video tests due to their artificial setup in a laboratory environment. Since they only assess isolated, partial performances, the results from video tests can be transferred to practical exercise scenarios only to a certain extent. However, game test situations are of high practical relevance since the test persons operate in quite realistic field conditions.

Figure 6.8 A standardised video test to measure tactical creativity in a laboratory setting in front of a large display

However, another advantage of video tests is that selected video sequences can be chosen and adjusted to relate to specific tactical decision performances. In game test situations, it is more difficult to prompt tactical actions by the test persons that cause only one isolated, tactical partial performance. For example, in the game test situation "Identification of Gaps", running into space and asking for the ball is restricted by the fact that every player has their set position which they must not leave. Another advantage of video tests is that through tactical responses, the test persons are forced to react to many different but comparable situations. In comparison, this can only be set up adequately in game test situations if the test persons operate for a long period of time (approximately fifteen minutes or more). By means of the respective adequate video sequences, a high consistency and thus a high reliability of the examined material can be guaranteed. Despite a consistent formulation of tasks, there will always be a certain amount of variability that can be optimised through an extension of the playing time in game test situations. This is a result of the natural conditions in game test situations. One last advantage of video tests is that one can easily add further manipulation stimuli (e.g. inducing motivational focus or attention directing instructions). Technically, this is also possible for game test situations; however, it is significantly harder to control.

Summary

In this chapter I described how tactical creativity can be evaluated in team and racket sports. Even though this is difficult, three possibilities currently exist. Game observation gives the opportunity to directly evaluate several tactical and creative solutions during a match. The difficulty is that some individual situations occur quite rarely. With the methodology of neuronal networks, it is possible not only to classify tactical patterns quickly and exactly, but also to extract original or rare solutions from the game as well. Laboratory video tests can be used to assess externally valid original solutions, but the artificial situation, in which solutions are assessed without physical motor action, limits the interpretability. Game test situations allow for the reliable and repeated emergence of tactical situations where players are able to show creative solutions. The advantages and disadvantages of the three possibilities in assessing creative solutions in team and racket sport are also discussed in detail.

Discussion questions

1   How can you measure tactical creativity in team sports like football or basketball without game test situations?
2   How can you measure tactical creativity with game test situations?
3   Which benefits do neuronal networks have when attempting to analyse tactical parameters like game development and wing play?
4   Try to develop new kinds of game test situations for "identification of gaps", "taking ball near goal" and "supporting and orienting" to access tactical creativity in other team and racket sports (cf. Chapter 5).

5   Try to develop new kinds of game test situations for other team and racket sports like baseball, American football, rugby or cricket.

6   Try to develop new kinds of game test situations for football using the group tactics in football from Chapter 5.

Additional reading

Memmert, D. (2010a) Testing of tactical performance in youth elite soccer. *Journal of Sports Science and Medicine*, 9, 199–205.

Memmert, D. (2010b) Creativity, expertise, and attention: Exploring their development and their relationships. *Journal of Sport Science*, 29, 93–104.

Memmert, D. (2013) Tactical creativity. In T. McGarry, P. O'Donoghue & J. Sampaio (eds.), *Routledge Handbook of Sports Performance Analysis* (pp. 297–308). Abingdon: Routledge.

Memmert, D. & Perl, J. (2009a) Game creativity analysis by means of neural networks. *Journal of Sport Science*, 27, 139–149.

Memmert, D. & Perl, J. (2009b) Analysis and simulation of creativity learning by means of artificial neural networks. *Human Movement Science*, 28, 263–282.

Oslin, J.L., Mitchell, S.A. & Griffin, L.L. (1998) The Game Performance Assessment Instrument (GPAI): Development and preliminary validation. *Journal of Teaching in Physical Education*, 17, 231–243.

7 Practical implications of the tactical creativity approach

The following three examples of teaching units demonstrate how teachers and coaches can foster tactical creativity in different basic tactical game forms. If a teacher wants to assess the divergent thinking performance of students, the behaviour of the players can be evaluated before and at the end of a teaching unit within Game Test Situations (see Chapter 6).

As explained in Chapter 6, the teacher or coach can evaluate three kinds of tactical behaviours of students:

> Originality – the teacher identifies any unusual and innovative ideas that only 10% produce (e.g. player throws the ball against the wall before it hits the ground; bounce pass through the leg of the defender; no-look pass).
> Fluency – the number of ideas will be counted during the task (Guilford, 1956; Torrance, 1988).
> Flexibility – the number of different kinds of ideas will be counted during the task (Torrance, 1988; Guilford, 1956).

In conclusion, the results may be averaged to get a final grade. The following teaching units demonstrate tactical creativity in 1-Dimension Games. These units teach how:

- Identification of gaps,
- Taking the ball near the goal, and
- Supporting and orienting

can be developed in accordance with the TCA model. That means:

- **Diversification**: Using different motor skills – left and right foot, hands, etc.
- **Deliberate coaching**: No tactical feedback, and no further tactical instructions; only the rules
- **Deliberate motivation**: Only promotion instructions

Teaching unit for developing tactical creativity in identification of gaps

This 1-**D**imension Game evokes tactical behaviour in the identification of gaps in recurring comparable situations (see Figure 7.1). Attackers 1, 2, 6 and 7 have the task of playing the ball past defenders 3, 4, and 5 and below the upper boundary into the opposite field. The players' aim is to find gaps and pass the ball through them.

Lesson 1

Lesson unit progression:

- Introduction of the task
- Performing the task using only hands
- Rotation of players (this means that positions and team players/opponents are systematically varied)

Lesson 2

Lesson unit progression:

- Performing the task using only feet
- Rotation of players

Lesson 3

Lesson unit progression:

- Performing the task with an implement (bigger ball)
- Rotation of players

Figure 7.1 1-**D**imension Game evokes tactical behaviour in the identification of gaps

Lesson 4

Lesson unit progression:

- Performing the task with the player's weak hand
- Rotation of players

Lesson 5

Lesson unit progression:

- Performing the task with the player's weak foot
- Rotation of players

Lesson 6

Lesson unit progression

- Performing the task with an implement (smaller ball)
- Rotation of players

Teaching unit for developing tactical creativity in taking the ball near the goal

This 1-Dimension Game can evoke tactical behaviour in "taking the ball near the goal" in recurring comparable situations (see Figure 7.2). Attackers 1, 2, 3 and 4 have the task of playing the ball past defenders 5 and 6 over the final line without losing the ball.

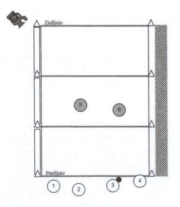 

Figure 7.2 1-**D**imension Game evokes tactical behaviour in taking the ball near the goal

Lesson 1

Lesson unit progression:

* Introduction of the task
* Performing the task using only hands
* Rotation of players (this means that positions and team players/opponents are systematically varied)

Lesson 2

Lesson unit progression:

* Performing the task using only feet
* Rotation of players

Lesson 3

Lesson unit progression:

* Performing the task with the implement (bigger ball)
* Rotation of players

Lesson 4

Lesson unit progression:

* Performing the task with the player's weak hand
* Rotation of players

Lesson 5

Lesson unit progression:

* Performing the task with the player's weak foot
* Rotation of players

Lesson 6

Lesson unit progression:

* Performing the task with an implement (smaller ball)
* Rotation of players

Teaching unit for developing tactical creativity in supporting and orienting

This 1-**D**imension Game can provoke tactical solutions in *off-the-ball movement* (orienting and supporting) in recurring comparable situations (see Figure 7.3). Attackers 1, 2 and 3 attempt to pass the ball among themselves as often as possible without defenders 4, 5 and 6 taking possession of the ball.

Lesson 1

Lesson unit progression:

* Introduction of the task
* Performing the task using only hands
* Rotation of players (this means that positions and team players/opponents are systematically varied)

Lesson 2

Lesson unit progression:

* Performing the task using only feet
* Rotation of players

Lesson 3

Lesson unit progression:

* Performing the task with an implement (bigger ball)
* Rotation of players

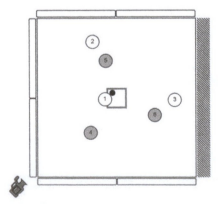 

Figure 7.3 1-**D**imension Game evokes tactical behaviour in supporting and orienting

Lesson 4

Lesson unit progression:

- Performing the task with the player's weak hand
- Rotation of players

Lesson 5

Lesson unit progression:

- Performing the task with the player's weak foot
- Rotation of players

Lesson 6

Lesson unit progression:

- Performing the task with an implement (smaller ball)
- Rotation of players

Summary

I described three 1-**D**imension Games to foster tactical creativity in identification of gaps, taking the ball near the goal, and supporting and orienting. In addition, three teaching units demonstrate how teachers and coaches can develop tactical creativity in accordance with the TCA model. Most importantly, rare, creative, flexible, and fluent tactical solutions should emerge from the students through these training units.

Discussion questions

1 How can the three game forms "identification of gaps", "taking the ball near the goal" and "supporting and orienting" be further differentiated to establish variations for the students?
2 Think of expanded and new forms of games to enhance tactical creativity which can train other individual basic tactics in team and racket sports.
3 Consider forms of games that pick out group basic tactics in football as a central theme for enhancing tactical creativity in football (cf. Chapter 5).
4 Which other game forms can be developed to implement the six **D**s from Chapter 5 into practical applications? In particular, think of game forms to widen the breadth of students' attention.

Additional reading

Griffin, L.A., Mitchell, S.A. & Oslin, J.L. (1997) *Teaching Sport Concepts and Skills: A Tactical Games Approach.* Champaign: Human Kinetics.

Memmert D. (2011) Sports and creativity. In M.A. Runco & S.R. Pritzker (eds.), *Encyclopedia of Creativity*, Second Edition, vol. 2, pp. 373–378. San Diego: Academic Press.

Memmert, D. & Harvey, S. (2010) Identification of non-specific tactical problems in invasion games. *Physical Education and Sport Pedagogy*, 15, 287–305.

Memmert, D. & König, S. (2007) Teaching games at elementary schools. *International Journal of Physical Education*, 44, 54–67.

8 Summary

Children are subject to a huge input of information within the blink of an eye in numerous team and racket sports. They must devote their attention to novel sensory impressions in the initial stages of the learning process, and they are required to maintain this alertness as they become increasingly advanced in team and racket sports. This raises the question of how developing players can heighten their ability to perceive changes in situations that demand skills extending beyond coached and practiced aspects of play. As it is impossible to recreate all the possible dynamics that may be encountered within a match, coaches are challenged to develop players' efficacy at identifying tactile solutions parallel to those previously practiced. Addressing these difficulties, this textbook ends with sport practical and theoretical implications of the TCA that may be important for trainers, coaches, and researchers.

Sport practical implications

The underlying question of this book was how and in what way coaches and teachers can elicit creative solutions from their players at certain, regular intervals. This is not only beneficial to team success but also for the children themselves, since in our society creative people are usually associated with character traits such as self-confidence, strength, and dominance (Barron, 1969). The cited findings from psychology, cognitive psychology, computer science in sports, and social psychology, as well as sport scientific result patterns from creativity research, offer a variety of ideas that could be implemented in sport clubs and school sport lessons. In summary, the key principles of developing tactical divergent thinking in team and racket sports are described in Table 8.1, and may be considered as first recommendations for sport lessons and training units (see also Figure 4.6).

On a practical level, the 6 **D**s and the results of experiments presented in Chapter 5 have implications for the design of tactically-oriented training programmes and curricula (Roth and Kröger, 2011; Memmert, Thumfart and Uhing, 2014; Mitchell, Oslin and Griffin, 2006; Roth, Kröger and Memmert, 2002; Roth, Memmert and Schubert, 2006). While environmental conditions are created and curriculum designs must be implemented that correspond to the

Table 8.1 The definition of the 6 **D**s of the TCA fostering tactical creativity

Deliberate-Play:	Uninstructed play without instructions or feedback can lead to trying out a multitude of different solutions.
1-Dimension-Games:	By means of multiple repetitions of similar situations, structured game forms can improve basic tactical skills across different sports with an amount of creative solutions.
Diversification:	Use of different motor skills in 1-**D**imension-Games can support the development of original solutions.
Deliberate-Coaching:	In 1-**D**imension-Games, no instructions shall be given that narrow the focus of attention of the acting players.
Deliberate-Motivation:	For 1-**D**imension-Games, promotion-instructions are to be given, to enlarge the generation of extraordinary solutions.
Deliberate-Practice:	In more advanced games, task-centered practice can lead to repeat and explore seldom but adequate solutions.

criteria of **D**iversification as well as **D**eliberate Play and **D**eliberate Practice, there are nevertheless additional methodological principles for conducting training units, like 1-**D**imension Games, breadth of attention, and promotion instructions.

Diversification, deliberate play, and deliberate practice

The results regarding the influence of the environment on fostering tactical creativity in professional life speak in favour of diverse training for children, or, with regard to scouting, the selection of players that have gained a multitude of different experiences in a great number of different team sports. For example, a late specialisation in especially team and racket sports would be desirable to foster tactical creativity. Other central aspects of this approach are a high number of different game forms and exercise variations, the initiation of diversified ways of movement, and a limited number of verbal instructions that could decrease the focus of attention. Therefore, children in their early years should not be subject to instruction-based and goal-oriented training. In fact, quite the opposite: to generate creative ideas, they should be provided with diversified ball material, as well as unstructured and sport-unspecific game forms (**D**eliberate Play). Later on, more and more structured and task-centred game forms have to be applied, to motivate the players specifically to apply learned solutions. Then, in later phases of childhood, convergent solutions in given situations have to be repeated and explored to develop a match plan for different kinds of solutions (**D**eliberate Practice).

1-Dimension games

During easy, algorithmic tasks, time can be saved through the use of automated solution routines (convergent thinking). When complex, imprecisely defined problems without concrete solutions present themselves, surprising and creative solutions can be the key to success (divergent thinking). Of course, this implies that in practice coaches and teachers are able to classify tasks according to their degree of complexity and to rate the expected solutions with regard to their costs and benefits. Initially 1-**D**imension Games have to be developed that train only one basic tactical competency. Later the 1-**D**imension Games can comprise various tactical competencies and become 2- or 3-**D**imension Games with multiple tactical dimensions. Independent of the number of tactical dimensions, 1-**D**imension Games can be as naturalistic and therefore as complex as possible.

Deliberate coaching

Attentional focus in team and racket sports can be controlled by a certain instructional design and by giving external information impulses. The central result of the **D**eliberate Coaching principle is that with substantial attention focus, unexpected and potentially more advantageous and appropriate solutions can be perceived, employed, and learned. Accordingly, attention plays a crucial role during the generation of original and creative solutions. For instance, distracting noises can lead to a reduced attention focus in children, which clearly impairs creative processes. Applied to the training of children and adolescents, these result patterns speak in favour of allowing all players a broad focus of attention, which can be better achieved when a limited number of calmly given instructions is presented instead of a multitude of loud commands.

One particular means to influence the focus of attention is the way instructions are given. Open considerations – instead of goal-oriented instructions that occupy the attention focus – lead to a higher probability of detecting unexpected objects and including them in possible solution processes. This way, more information will be represented by a person, which can then be combined and may be advantageous for the generation of unexpected and novel solutions. Creativity can therefore be said to thrive from *freedom* rather than from *instructions*.

Deliberate motivation

The central point of communication processes of coaches and teachers should therefore be the use of reward contingencies, i.e. the prospect of winning or not winning instead of losing or not losing. Announcements of coaches and teachers should therefore sound like this: "You are more likely to play in the starting team when you solve this task, and you will be less likely to play when you don't solve this task successfully" – and not like this: "Your chance to make it to the starting team decreases when you don't solve this task successfully, but you will probably be in the starting team when you solve this task successfully."

The emotional state of a person plays an important role when solving any kind of task. Whenever there are free and joyful working conditions, positive effects on creativity can be assumed through independence, the willingness to take risks, and the expectation of success. Furthermore, it is possible to positively influence cognitive performance through the use of particular emotion-inducing stimuli. A promotion focus enhances divergent tactical solution strategies whereas a prevention focus entails a better performance in convergent tactical tasks. Depending on the type of task and the solution expected by a coach or teacher, different instructions should be given.

Theoretical implications

It has become clear that:

a) creative processes are very complex by nature,
b) not all results from scientific studies can directly be transferred to ecologically valid situations,
c) there are no developed, simple formulas that guarantee a constant development of spontaneous creative ideas.

Nevertheless, the results of the studies described in Chapter 5 can be integrated into the theoretical framework developed by Sternberg and Lubart (1991). The fundamental result is a novel and preliminary test of comprehensive resources for creative performance in the domain of sports. Through this theoretical framework, it becomes clear that resources, attention, expertise, environment, and motivation are important in finding original solutions to complex situations in sports. Moreover, intellectual style and personality may be further implicated in the optimisation of divergent tactical performance in sports. With regard to attention research, the majority of the described studies are based on the Inattentional Blindness Paradigm. As such, their results provide further insight into the description and validation of inattentional blindness via extensions of the paradigm to situational characteristics (complexity, instructions, motivational framing) and personality characteristics (expertise, age, giftedness, chronic promotion/ prevention focus).

Furthermore, a connection to the generation of original and versatile solution possibilities is achievable. Further specific theoretical implications can be derived from individual studies that parallel the resources referred to above. The findings derived from these studies highlight the fact that the Inattentional Blindness paradigm also appears to play a considerable role in competitive sports. Team players often fail to find an optimal tactical solution to a situation because the coach has narrowed their focus of attention through restrictive instructions. However, team members can capture the attention of other teammates by waving their hands as important meaningful exogenous stimuli. This led to a major reduction in inattentional blindness (cf. the results of Memmert and Furley, 2007).

These findings show that current theories in the field of neuropsychology have explanatory potential in particularly complex contexts. Enactive theories make stronger use of preconscious self-organising processes which precede every state of awareness in the cortex, and attempt to optimise this resulting state for functional purposes.

Before conscious knowledge of the observed object is available, self-organised processes influence the direction of attention through potentially useful or emotionally interesting information (Ellis, 2001). This is possible since cognitive functions are connected with emotional areas of the brain early in processing. This indicates that after the information passes from the optic nerve to the thalamus, the thalamus and the limbic system act together before V1 (area of the visual cortex that receives input) to V4 (area of the visual cortex that puts out information) are integrated (e.g. Watt, 2000). Through this mechanism the direction of attention is controlled and the information process is influenced by motivational factors before the organism consciously perceives the specific input. Ellis (2001) substantiated these enactive theories with neuropsychological discoveries (Ellis and Newton, 2000) and findings from inattentional blindness studies (Mack and Rock, 1998). These authors revealed a significant reduction in inattentional blindness in static settings if an emotional stimulus (e.g. ☺ vs. ☻; 85% vs. 15% noticing rate) was given. Another example of emotional stimuli is important words, such as the first name of participants, which were detected significantly more often than the two most frequently used words in America, "house" (88%) or "time" (50%).

The neuropsychological findings of Ellis (2001) used an extrapolated, three-tiered model. The first stage of this model is a "pre-selective" evaluation of stimuli determined by categories which are emotionally useful. A self-organising process is considered by Ellis (2001, p. 315) as a kind of early "penstock-mechanism". It is possible that this mechanism favours important or emotionally interesting information for further processing. In the second stage, stimuli that passed the pre-selection are "amplified", further processed, and encoded. In the third stage, consciousness is generated through resonance between anterior and posterior attention-mechanisms. This suggests that these cognitive processes can take part both in the early selection of incoming stimuli as well as in determining the information that later reaches consciousness. Nevertheless, whether information reaches consciousness or not is considered to be specified to a great extent by an early processing stage. Enactive theories demonstrate that the mechanisms of early and late selection are employed and controlled by the same subcortical and limbic processes.

Within the scope of the Inattentional Blindness Paradigm, it would be an important additional validation to show that blindness through inattention is a universal occurrence. Currently, there are no psychological studies supporting this claim. For sports sciences in particular, this finding would mean that inattentional blindness is detectable independently of a specific player position. Currently, blindness through inattention has only been documented from the perspective of the back area player in handball and the playmaker in basketball. What is the significance of the perspective of a pivot player or wing player in handball, a centre in basketball, or a goalkeeper in football or hockey? In order to understand inattentional blindness as a specific awareness phenomenon and as an overlapping ability, it is necessary to empirically validate its generalities in parallel situations.

Breadth of attention is the term used to refer to the number and range of stimuli that a subject attends to at any one time. The research presented in Chapter 5 supported the view that fewer instructions by coaches during game play lead to a wider breadth of attention, thereby facilitating greater improvements in tactical creativity (Memmert, 2007). These findings support previous research on attention-narrowing environment stimulations (Dewing and Battye, 1971; Friedman, Fishbach, Förster and Werth, 2003; Mendelsohn, 1976; Mendelsohn and Griswold, 1964, 1966; Martindale, 1999; for a review see Kasof, 1997) which found, on the one hand, that a narrow breadth of attention limits the amount of stimuli and information that can be taken in and associated, reducing the potential of discovering unique and original solutions. On the other hand, however, a wide breadth of attention makes it possible to associate different stimuli that may initially appear to be irrelevant. Considered together, the findings highlight the fact that using an attention-broadening programme can be advantageous in promoting the development of creativity in children. This programme appears to be particularly suitable for achieving a wide breadth of attention during game play. Martindale (1981, p. 372) explains this fact in the following statement:

"The more elements that a person can focus on simultaneously, the more likely it is that a creative idea will result. Why? Because the more elements that can be focused on, the more candidates there are for combination. Thus, with two elements – A and B – in the focus of attention, only one relationship – AB – can be discovered. With three elements – A, B, and C – there are three potential relationships – AB, AC, and BC – to be discovered. With four elements, there are six potential relationships, and so on."

In order to replicate the current findings under ecologically valid circumstances, one would have to analyse tactical decision-making changes while participants carry out their decisions physically (i.e. not only mentally play the pass to player X, but really play it). Furthermore, the ability to replicate experimental results in real-life situations, for example sports competitions, remains unexamined. Obtaining such results would require either the development of explicit scripts for the players, or an analysis of authentic and uncontrolled sports recordings. The latter could be performed by analysing authentic recordings from a first person perspective under rigid guidelines from a coach. The resolution of these issues could provide a more comprehensive model of sport decision making, especially in divergent tactical thinking.

Another type of research shows that different environmental influences and organisational conditions enhance the generation of original thinking, a finding especially validated in studies of prominent athletes (Memmert, Baker and Bertsch, 2010). While socially characterised external circumstances largely cannot be influenced directly, training options for youth can be targeted and controlled. For example, children are missing the natural experience of playing in the streets that is essential for their creative development (Roth, 2005), but this lack can be compensated by access to team ball sports spanning all games, as is practiced in the "Ball School Heidelberg" (Roth and Kröger, 2011; Roth, Kröger and Memmert, 2002; Roth, Memmert and Schubert, 2006). It has been shown that general and versatile training ("diversification") directly affects the divergent tactical development of children (cf. Memmert and Roth, 2007). At the same time, it was shown that exceptional and creative athletes in basketball, football, handball and hockey had competed far more often and more intensely without guidance in many relatively unstructured and complex team ball sports situations ("Deliberate Play") in their early youth (up to age fourteen) than less talented team players. In addition, exceptional athletes have also trained significantly longer and more purposefully in their main sport than less creative top athletes ("Deliberate Practice"). This evidence therefore provides a basis for the convergence of the two prevalent research programmes, expertise research and creativity research, that have not been discussed in the same context so far. Both results suggest that practice experiences and early play are important influences on the development of sport creativity. In this case, specific experiences over a long time (the ten-year rule; Ericsson, Krampe and Tesch-Römer, 1993; but see Macnamara et al., 2014) are necessary for the attainment of expertise (e.g. Helsen, Starkes and Hodges, 1998; Kalinowski, 1985; Monsaas, 1985). Additionally, current theoretical approaches and empirical research regarding the development of creativity (Csikszentmihalyi, 1999; Kurtzberg and Amabile, 2000–2001; Martindale, 1990; Milgram, 1990; Smith, Ward and Finke, 1995; Sternberg and Lubart, 1995) support the view that gathering diversified and non-specific experiences (such as unstructured play) over the course of multiple years is an ideal medium for the development of creative thinking.

Theoretical extensions of the two resources of motivation and personality seem premature at this point. However, it may be noted that personality variables in connection with motivational instructions (promotion/prevention framing) have a direct effect on technical/tactical and even creative performance in team sports (Memmert et al., 2013). Such considerations have potential for optimising divergent tactical performances in racket sports, too.

Numerous experiments from social psychology argue compellingly that instructions promoting a happy mood or a promotion focus can facilitate creative performance or creative solutions (for an overview see Isen, 2000; see also Chapter 5). It is desirable that sports science will, in ecological settings, contribute to the further development of motivationally-oriented theoretic models from social psychology (e.g. Regulatory Focus Theory, Higgins, 1997; Theory of Personality Systems Interactions, Kuhl, 2000), whose discussion and empirical investigation is at a comparatively early stage (Aspinwall, 1998; Derryberry and Tucker, 1994; Fredrickson, 2001; Isen, 2000).

Essential to this discussion are further additional theoretical research questions that require clarification. The largest gain of insight is expected from future research and experimental examination of the attentional theories investigating the link between motivation and creativity. Unconscious processes act as early selection mechanisms that favour useful or emotionally interesting information for further processing. Motivational factors therefore control the direction of attention and influence information processing before the organism consciously perceives the specific input. Still unanswered is the main question of which motivational usefulness categories exist. Ellis (2001, p. 314) names three types of stimuli to address this topic. They all have a sound evolutionary basis: a) emotionally salient, b) meaningful, c) presence as part of the human hardware (e.g. loud noise). Are there "pre-information" cues that could help team sport players to pick up relevant information in novel and unexpected situations? For instance, a novel situation can occur when a previously marked player releases himself from his opponent by making a feint. Meaningful stimuli can be detected by players with the assistance of motivational usefulness categories. The visual or conceptual image scheme is formed by these "search activities" (Ellis, 2001) before occipital activity takes effect on perceptive awareness.

Besides this, the TCA makes a step towards integrating different paradigms on human cognition and action in sports, defined as cognitive and dynamical systems approaches. In my opinion these paradigms have more common ground than is usually recognised, and a unification of vocabulary, or at least the possibility for translation, can reduce the explanatory gaps that exist in both of them individually, and can reinforce their synergistic effect with respect to their research scope. In other words, the objective of my theoretical platform of TCA is to serve as a multidisciplinary system of integrating ideas, producing synthesised knowledge about the processes of perception, cognition and action in everyday activities for the development of an alternative paradigm for theory, practice, and research in the behavioural sciences, especially sports.

Over recent years there has been an increasing demand for installing interdisciplinary projects all over the world which bring colleagues from different fields of research into collaboration. This move is based on the expectation that new results, even in individual disciplines, depend more and more on a fruitful transfer of knowledge. It is particularly to be expected that in the case of well-structured and successfully run research paradigms, additional potential is available from interdisciplinary collaboration – specfically by a creative exchange of methods and ideas.

Summary

In Chapter 8, the final sport practical and theoretical implications for team and racket sports are summarised and discussed in detail. It is possible for teachers and coaches to resort to the 6 **Ds** to support the development of original solutions in different kinds of sports.

In uninstructed tactical play situations (**Deliberate** play) with 1-**Dimension** Games, it is possible to improve basic tactical skills across different sports. **Diversification** of different motor skills should be used, and **Deliberate Coaching** means less instruction is needed to provoke a wide breadth of attention to perceive greater amounts of information which could be important for decision-making. **Deliberate Motivation** is defined as giving promotion instructions to foster the generation of creative solutions. Finally, only for more advanced children does

Deliberate Practice become more and more important. As in all research programmes, many questions are left open and as yet unanswered. Some suggestions for future research perspectives were discussed, which should be pursued theoretically and empirically. However, I believe that a first step has been taken in this book. I showed on the one hand that tactical creativity can be trained and is not solely based on genius, and on the other hand, that tactical creativity in team and racket sports can be fostered. After the US-American writer Ambrose Bierce, we want to conclude that now we coaches and teachers know a little more, but still we admit to modesty, because we know that this is just the beginning: "Knowledge is what we call the small part of the lack of knowledge that we ordered."

Discussion questions

1   Summarize the 6 **Ds** of TCA and choose a sport where you set up training units with which you can foster tactical creativity with reference to the 6 **Ds** of TCA.
2   Critically discuss the connection between attention processes and emotions in light of the neuro-scientific framework.
3   Identify important issues regarding tactical creativity that have to be answered in future research projects in sports science.
4   Which ideas can you take from the TCA, which will help you to produce original ideas for certain problems in living?

Additional reading

Barron, F. (1969) *Creative Person and Creative Process*. Montreal: Holt, Rinehart and Winston.
Ellis, R.D. (2001) Implication of inattentional blindness for "enactive" theories of consciousness. *Brain and Mind*, 2, 297–322.
Ericsson, K.A., Krampe, R. & Tesch-Römer, C. (1993) The role of deliberate practice in the acquisition of expert performance. *Psychological Review*, 100, 363–406.
Helsen, W.F., Starkes, J.L. & Hodges, N.J. (1998) Team sports and the theory of deliberate practice. *Journal of Sport and Exercise Psychology*, 20, 12–34.
Kasof, J. (1997) Creativity and breadth of attention. *Creativity Research Journal*, 10, 303–315.
Macnamara, B.N., Hambrick, D.Z. & Oswald, F.L. (2014). Deliberate Practice and Performance in Music, Games, Sports, Education, and Professions A Meta-Analysis. *Psychological Science*, 25, 1608–1618.
Memmert, D. (2011) Sports and Creativity. In M.A. Runco & S.R. Pritzker (eds.), *Encyclopedia of Creativity,* Second Edition, vol. 2, pp. 373–378. San Diego: Academic Press.
Werth, L. & Förster, J. (2007b) Regulatorischer Fokus. Ein Überblick. *Zeitschrift für Sozialpsychologie*, 38, 33–42.

References

Abernethy, B., Baker, J. & Côté, J. (2005) Transfer of pattern recall skills may contribute to the development of sport expertise. *Applied Cognitive Psychology*, 19, 705–718.

Almond, L. (1986) Reflecting on themes: A games classification. In R. Thorpe, D. Bunker & L. Almond (eds.), *Rethinking Games Teaching* (p. 71–72). Loughborough: University of Technology.

Alvarez, G.A. & Franconeri, S.L. (2005) How many objects can you track? Evidence for a flexit tracking resource. *Journal of Vision*, 5, 641.

Amabile, T.M. (1983) Social psychology of creativity: A componential conceptualization. *Journal of Personality and Social Psychology*, 45, 357–376.

Amabile, T.M. (1996) *Creativity in Context*. Boulder, CO: Westview Press.

Amelang, M. & Bartussek, D. (2006) *Differenzielle Psychologie und Persönlichkeitsforschung*. Stuttgart: Kohlhammer.

Araújo, D., Davids, K., Bennett, S., Button, C. & Chapman, G. (2004) Emergence of sport skills under constraints. In A.M. Williams & N.J. Hodges (eds.), *Skill Acquisition in Sport: Research, theory and practice* (pp. 409–434). London: Routledge.

Araujo, D., Davids, K. & Hristovski, R. (2006) The ecological dynamics of decision making in sport. *Psychology of Sport and Exercise*, 7, 653–676.

Araújo, D., Davids, K. & Serpa, S. (2005) An ecological approach to expertise effects in decision-making in a simulated sailing regatta. *Psychology of Sport and Exercise*, 6, 671–692.

Arend, S. (1980) Developing perceptual skills prior to motor performance. *Motor Skills*, 4, 11–17.

Ashby, G.F., Valentin, V.V. & Turken, A.U. (2002) The effects of positive affect and arousal on working memory and executive attention: Neurobiology and computational models. In S. Moore & M. Oaksford (eds.), *Emotional Cognition: From brain to behaviour* (pp. 245–287). Amsterdam: Benjamins.

Aspinwall, L.G. (1998) Rethinking the role of positive effect in self-regulation. *Motivation and Emotion*, 23, 1–23.

Baca, A., Dabnichki, P., Heller, M. & Kornfeind, P. (2009) Ubiquitous computing in sports: A review and analysis. *Journal of Sports Sciences*, 27, 1135–1346.

Bailey, R. & Kirk, D. (eds.) (2009) *The Routledge Physical Education Reader*. Oxford: Routledge.

Baker, J. (2003) Early specialization in youth sport: A requirement for adult expertise? *High Ability Studies*, 14, 85–92.

Baker, J., Côté, J. & Abernethy, B. (2003) Sport specific training, deliberate practice and the development of expertise in team ball sports. *Journal of Applied Sport Psychology*, 15, 12–25.

Bakker, F.C., Whiting, H.T.A. & Van der Burg, H. (1990) *Sport Psychology: Concepts and application*. Lanchester: Butties.

Bardy, B.G. (2004) Postural coordination dynamics in standing humans. In V.K. Jirsa and J.A.S. Kelso (eds.), *Coordination Dynamics: Issues and Trends, Applied Complex Systems* (pp. 103–121). New York: Springer Verlag.

Bardy, B.G., Marin, L., Stoffregen, T.A. & Bootsma, R.J. (1999) Postural coordination modes considered as emergent phenomena. *Journal of Experimental Psychology: Human Perception and Performance*, 25, 1284–1301.

Barron, F. (1965) The psychology of creativity. In T.M. Newcomb (ed.), *New Directions in Psychology II*. New York: Rinehart.

Barron, F. (1969) *Creative Person and Creative Process*. Montreal: Holt, Rinehart and Winston.

Battig, W.F. (1966) Evidence for coding processes in "rote" paired-associate learning. *Journal of Verbal Learning and Verbal Behaviour*, 5, 177–181.

Beard, C.H. (1993) Transfer of computer skills from introductory computer courses. *Journal of Research in Computing Education*, 25, 423–430.

Beckmann, H., Winkel, C. & Schöllhorn, W.I. (2010) Optimal range of variation in hockey technique training. *International Journal of Sports Psychology*, 41, 5–10.

Bennis, W., Heil, G. & Stephens, D.C. (2000) *Douglas McGregor, Revisited: Managing the human side of the enterprise*. New York: John Wiley & Sons.

Berry, D.C. & Broadbent, D.E. (1988) Interactive tasks and the implicit-explicit distinction. *British Journal of Psychology*, 79, 251–272.

Boden, M.A. (2003) Computer Models of Creativity. In R.J. Sternberg (ed.), *Handbook of Creativity* (pp. 351–372). Cambridge: Cambridge University Press.

Boekaerts, M. (1999) Self-regulated learning: Where we are today. *International Journal of Educational Research*, 31 (6), 445–457.

Brauna, J. & Mattia, M. (2010) Attractors and noise: Twin drivers of decisions and multistability. *NeuroImage*, 52, 740–775.

Brunswik, E. (1955) Representative design and probabilistic theory in a functional psychology. *Psychological Review*, 62, 193–217.

Bunker, D. & Thorpe, R. (1982) A model for the teaching of games in secondary schools. *Bulletin of Physical Education*, 18, 5–8.

Button, C., Dicks, M., Haines, R., Barker, R. & Davids, K. (2011) Statistical modelling of gaze behaviour as categorical time series: What you should watch to save soccer penalties. *Cognitive Processing*, 112, 235–244.

Cabeza, R. & Nyberg, L. (2000) Imaging cognition II: An empirical review of 275 PET and fMRI studies. *Journal of Cognitive Neuroscience*, 12, 1–47.

Cattell, R.B. (1971) *Abilities: Their structure, growth and action*. Boston: Haughton Mifflin.

Chabris, C.F., Weinberger, A., Fontaine, M. & Simons, D.J. (2011) You do not talk about Fight Club if you do not notice Fight Club: Inattentional blindness for a simulated real-world assault. *i-Perception*, 2, 150.

Chapman, J.A. (1978) Playfulness and the development of divergent thinking abilities. *Child: Care, Health and Development*, 4, 371–83.

Chen, W. & Rovegno, I. (2000) Examination of expert and novice teachers' constructivist-oriented teaching practices using a movement approach to elementary physical education. *Research Quarterly for Exercise and Sport,* 71, 357–372.

Chiviacowsky, S. & Wulf, G. (2002) Self-controlled feedback: Does it enhance learning because performers get feedback when they need it? *Research Quarterly for Exercise and Sport,* 73, 408–415.

Chow, J.Y., Davids, K., Button, C., Shuttleworth, R., Renshaw, I. & Araújo, D. (2007) The role of nonlinear pedagogy in physical education. *Review of Educational Research,* 77, 251–278.

Cleeremans, A., Destrebecqz, A. & Boyer, M. (1998) Implicit learning: News from the front. *Trends in Cognitive Sciences,* 2, 406–416.

Clemente, F., Couceiro, M., Martins, F.M.L. & Mendes, R. (2012) The usefulness of small-sided games on soccer training. *Journal of Physical Education and Sport,* 12, 93–102.

Čoh, M., Jovanović-Golubović, D. & Bratić, M. (2004) Motor learning in sport. *Physical Education and Sport,* 2, 45–59.

Cohen, A., Ivry, R. & Keele, S.W. (1990) Attention and structure in sequence learning. *Journal of Experimental Psychology: Learning, Memory, and Cognition,* 16, 17–30.

Côté, J. & Hay, J. (2002) Children's involvement in sport: A developmental perspective. In J. Silva & D. Stevens (eds.), *Psychological Foundations of Sport* (pp. 484–502). Boston, MA: Merrill.

Côté, J., Baker, J. & Abernethy, B. (2003) From play to practice: A developmental framework for the acquisition of expertise in team sports. In J.L. Starkes & K.A. Ericsson (eds.), *Recent Advances in Research on Sport Expertise* (pp. 89–110). Champaign, IL: Human Kinetics.

Côté, J., Baker, J. & Abernethy, B. (2007) Play and practice in the development of sport expertise. In G. Tenenbaum & R.C. Eklund (eds.), *Handbook of Sport Psychology* (pp. 184–202). Hoboken, NJ: Wiley.

Cropley, A. (1995) Kreativität. In M. Amelang (ed.), *Verhaltens- und Leistungsunterschiede. Themenbereich C. Serie VIII, Bd. 2* (pp. 329–373). Göttingen: Hogrefe.

Csikszentmihalyi, M. (1988) Society, culture, and person: A systems view of creativity. In R.J. Sternberg (ed.), *The Nature of Creativity* (pp. 325–339). New York: Cambridge University Press.

Csikszentmihalyi, M. (1999) Creativity. In R.A. Wilson & F.C. Keil (eds.), *The MIT Encyclopedia of the Cognitive Sciences* (pp. 205–206). Cambridge: MIT Press.

Cummings, M.L. & Tsonis, C.G. (2005) *Deconstructing complexity in air traffic control.* HFES Annual Conference, Orlando, FL (unpublished paper).

Damasio, A.R. (2001) Some notes on brain, imagination and creativity. In K.H. Pfenninger & V.R. Shubik (eds.), *The Origins of Creativity* (pp. 59–68). Oxford: Oxford University Press.

Daugs, R. (1978) Bewegungslehre zwischen Biomechanik und Kybernetik. Wissenschaftstheoretische Überlegungen zu einer komplex-wissenschaftlichen Bewegungslehre. *Sportwissenschaft,* 1, 69–90.

Davids, K., Button, C. & Bennett, S. (2008) *Dynamics of Skill Acquisition: A constraints-led approach.* Champaign, IL: Human Kinetics.

Deco, G., Jirsa, V.K., Robinson, P.A., Breakspear, M. & Friston, K. (2008) The dynamic brain: From spiking neurons to neural masses and cortical fields. *PLOS Computational Biology,* 4. (doi:10.1371/journal.pcbi.1000092.)

Deco, G., Rolls, E.T., Albantakis, L. & Romo, R. (2013) Brain mechanisms for perceptual and reward-related decision-making. *Progress in Neurobiology,* 103, 194–213.

De Dreu, C.K., Nijstad, B.A., Baas, M., Wolsink, I. & Roskes, M. (2012) Working memory benefits creative insight, musical improvisation, and original ideation through maintained task-focused attention. *Personality and Social Psychology Bulletin*, 38, 656–669.

Den Duyn, N. (1997) *Game Sense: Developing thinking players*. Belconnen, ACT Australia: Australian Sports Commission.

Derryberry, D. & Tucker, D.M. (1994) Motivating the focus of attention. In P.M. Niedenthal & S. Kitayama (eds.), *Heart's Eye: Emotional influences in perception and attention* (pp. 167–196). New York: Academic Press.

Dewing, K. & Battye, G. (1971) Attention deployment and non-verbal fluency. *Journal of Personality and Social Psychology*, 17, 214–218.

Dicks, M., Button, C. & Davids, K. (2010) Examination of gaze behaviors under in situ and video simulation task constraints reveals differences in information pickup for perception and action. *Attention, Perception, and Psychophysics*, 772, 706–720.

Dietrich, A. (2004) Neurocognitive mechanisms underlying the experience of flow. *Consciousness and Cognition*, 13, 746–761.

Dodds, P., Griffin, L.L. & Placek, J.H. (2001) A selected review of the literature on development of learners' domain-specific knowledge. *Journal of Teaching in Physical Education*, 20, 301–313.

Dohmen, T.J. (2008) Do professionals choke under pressure? *Journal of Economic Behaviour and Organization*, 65, 636–653.

Domjan, M. (2008) Adaptive specializations and generality of the laws of classical and instrumental conditioning. In R. Menzel & J. Byrne (eds.). *Learning Theory and Behaviour*. Vol. 1 of *Learning and Memory: A comprehensive reference* pp. (327–340). Oxford: Elsevier.

Drew, T., Võ, M.L.H. & Wolfe, J.M. (2013) The invisible gorilla strikes again: Sustained inattentional blindness in expert observers. *Psychological Science*, 1–6. doi:10.1177/0956797613479386.

Edelman, G.M. & Gally, J.A. (2001) Degeneracy and complexity in biological systems. *Proceedings of the National Academy of Sciences*, 98, 13763–13768.

Edelman, G.M. & Gally, J.A. (2013) Reentry: A key mechanism for integration of brain function. *Frontiers in Integrative Neuroscience*, 7. (Doi: 10.3389/fnint.2013.00063.)

Ekvall, G. & Ryhammer, L. (1999) The creative climate: Its determinants and effects at a Swedish University. *Creativity Research Journal*, 12, 303–310.

Ellis, R.D. (2001) Implication of inattentional blindness for "enactive" theories of consciousness. *Brain and Mind*, 2, 297–322.

Ellis, R.D. & Newton, N. (eds.) (2000) *The Cauldron of Consciousness: Affect, Motivation, and Self-organization*. Amsterdam: John Benjamins.

Elsner, B. & Hommel, B. (2001) Effect anticipation and action control. *Journal of Experimental Psychology: Human Perception and Performance*, 27, 229–240.

Ericsson, K.A., Krampe, R. & Tesch-Römer, C. (1993) The role of deliberate practice in the acquisition of expert performance. *Psychological Review*, 100, 363–406.

Farrow, D. & Abernethy, B. (2002) Can anticipatory skills be learned through implicit video-based perceptual training? *Journal of Sports Sciences*, 20, 471–485.

Fink, A. & Benedek, M (2013). The creative brain: brain correlates underlying the generation of original ideas. In: O. Vartanian, A.S. Bristol, & J.C. Kaufman (Eds.), *Neuroscience of creativity* (pp. 207–232). Cambridge: MIT press.

Fink, A., Grabner, R.H., Benedek, M., Reishofer, G., Hauswirth, V., Fally, M., Neuper, C., Ebner, F. & Neubauer, A.C. (2009) The creative brain: Investigation of brain activity during creative problem solving by means of EEG and fMRI. *Human Brain Mapping*, 30, 734–748.

Fink, A., Graif, B. & Neubauer, A.C. (2009) Brain correlates underlying creative thinking: EEG alpha activity in professional vs. novice dancers. *NeuroImage,* 46, 854–862.

Florida, R. (2002) *The Rise of the Creative Class*. New York: Basic Books.

Florida, R. & Tinagli, I. (2004) *Europe in the Creative Age*. London: Demos Publications.

Frank, T.D., Michelbrink, M., Beckmann, H. and Schöllhorn, W.I. (2008) A quantitative dynamical systems approach to differential learning: Self-organization principle and order parameter equations. *Biological Cybernetics*, 98, 19–31.

Franks, I. (1985) Qualitative and quantitative analysis. *Coaching Review*, 8, 48–50.

Fredrickson, B.L. (2001) The role of positive emotions in positive psychology: The broaden and build theory of positive emotions. *American Psychologist*, 56, 218–226.

French, K.E. & Thomas, J.R. (1987) The relation of knowledge development to children's basketball performance. *Journal of Sport Psychology*, 9, 15–32.

French, K.E., Werner, P.H., Rink, J.E., Taylor, K. & Hussey, K. (1996a) The effects of a 3-week unit of tactical, skill or combined tactical and skill instruction on badminton performance of ninth-grade students. *Journal of Teaching in Physical Education*, 15, 418–438.

French, K.E., Werner, P.H., Taylor, K., Hussey, K. & Jones, J. (1996b) The effects of a 6-week unit of tactical, skill, or combined tactical and skill instruction on badminton performance of ninth-grade-students. *Journal of Teaching in Physical Education*, 15, 439–463.

Friedman, R.S. & Förster, J. (2000) The effects of approach and avoidance motor actions on the elements of creative insight. *Journal of Personality and Social Psychology*, 79 (4), 477–492.

Friedman, R.S., Fishbach, A., Förster, J. & Werth, L. (2003) Attentional priming effects on creativity. *Creativity Research Journal*, 15, 277–286.

Friedman, R.S. & Förster, J. (2001) The effects of promotion and prevention cues on creativity. *Journal of Personality and Social Psychology*, 81, 1001–1013.

Fritzke, B. (1997) A self-organizing network that can follow non-stationary distributions. In *Proceedings of ICANN97, International Conference on Artificial Neural Networks*, 613–618.

Furley, P., Memmert, D. & Heller, C. (2010) The dark side of visual awareness in sport: Inattentional blindness in a real-world basketball task. *Attention, Perception, and Psychophysics*, 72, 1327–1337.

Gabbett, T. (2006) Skill-based conditioning games as an alternative to traditional conditioning for rugby league players. *Journal of Strength Conditioning Research*, 20, 309–315.

Gabbett, T., Jenkins, D. & Abernethy, B. (2009) Game-based training for improving skill and physical fitness in team sport athletes. *International Journal of Sports Science Coaching*, 4, 273–283.

Gabriele, T.E., Lee, T.D. & Hall, C.R. (1991) Contextual interference in movement timing: Specific effects in retention and transfer. *Journal of Human Movement Studies*, 20, 177–188.

Garaigordobil, M. & Berrueco, L. (2011) Effects of a play program on creative thinking of preschool children. *Spanish Journal of Psychology*, 14, 608–618.

Gardner, H. (1993) *Multiple Intelligences: The theory in practice*. New York: Basic Books.

Garrett, H.E. (1946) Developmental theory of intelligence. *American Psychologist*, 1, 372–378.

Getzels, J. W. & Csikszentmihalyi, M. (1976) *The Creative Vision: A longitudinal study of problem finding in art.* New York: Wiley.

Ginsburg, G.P. & Whittemore, R.G. (1968) Creativity and verbal ability: A direct examination of their relationship. *British Journal of Educational Psychology, 38,* 133–139.

Goode, S. & Magill, R.A. (1986) Contextual interference effects in learning three badminton serves. *Research Quarterly for Exercise and Sport*, 57, 308–314.

Gordon, W. (1961) *Synectics: The development of creative capacity.* New York: Harper and Row.

Gorman, A.D., Abernethy, B. & Farrow, D. (2013) The expert advantage in dynamic pattern recall persists across both attended and unattended display elements. *Attention, Perception, and Psychophysics*, 75, 835–844.

Graham, K.C., Ellis, S.D., Williams, D.C., Kwak, E.C. & Werner, P.H. (1996) High- and low-skilled target students' academic achievement and instructional performance in a 6-week badminton unit. *Journal of Teaching in Physical Education*, 15, 477–489.

Greco, P., Memmert, D. & Morales, J.C.P. (2010) The effect of deliberate play on tactical performance in basketball. *Perceptual and Motor Skills*, 110, 849–856.

Green, C.S. & Bavelier, D. (2003) Action video game modifies visual selective attention. *Nature*, 423, 534–537.

Gréhaigne, J.F., Godbout, P. & Bouthier, D. (1997) Performance assessment in team sports. *Journal of Teaching in Physical Education*, 16, 500–516.

Gréhaigne, J.F., Godbout, P. & Bouthier, D. (1999) The foundations of tactics and strategy in team sports. *Journal of Teaching in Physical Education*, 18, 159–174.

Gréhaigne, J.F., Wallian, N. & Godbout, P. (2005) Tactical-decision learning model and students' practices. *Physical Education and Sport Pedagogy*, 10, 255–269.

Griffin, L.A., Mitchell, S.A. & Oslin, J.L. (1997) *Teaching Sport Concepts and Skills: A Tactical Games Approach.* Champaign: Human Kinetics.

Grimm, L., Markman, A., Maddox, W. & Baldwin, G. (2008) Differential effects of regulatory fit on category learning. *Journal of Experimental Social Psychology, 44,* 920–927.

Grunz, A., Memmert, D. & Perl, J. (2012) Tactical pattern recognition in soccer games by means of special self-organizing maps. *Human Movement Science*, 31, 334–343.

Grunz, A., Memmert, D. & Perl, J. (2009) Analysis and simulation of actions in games by means of special self-organizing maps. *International Journal of Computer Science in Sport,* 8, 22–36.

Guilford, J.P. (1956) The structure of intellect. *Psychological Bulletin*, 53, 267–293.

Guilford, J.P. (1967) *The Nature of Human Intelligence.* New York: McGraw Hill.

Haddon, F.A. & Lytton, H. (1968) Teaching approach and the development of divergent thinking abilities in primary schools. *British Journal of Educational Psychology*, 38, 171–180.

Haken, H. (2000) *Information and Self-Organization: A macroscopic approach to complex systems.* Heidelberg: Springer.

Haken, H., Kelso, J.S. & Bunz, H. (1985) A theoretical model of phase transitions in human hand movements. *Biological Cybernetics*, 51, 347–356.

Hall, K.G. & Magill, R.A. (1995) Variability of practice and contextual interference in motor skill learning. *Journal of Motor Behaviour*, 27, 299–309.

Hamsen, G., Greco, P. & Samulski, D. (2000) Biographies of highly creative Brazilian and German team sport players.*Unpublished project report, Heidelberg.*

Handford, C., Davids, K., Bennett, S. & Button, C. (1997) Skill acquisition in sport: Some applications of an evolving practice ecology. *Journal of Sports Sciences*, 15, 621–640.

Harvey, L. & Anderson, J. (1996) Transfer of declarative knowledge in complex information-processing domains. *Human-Computer Interaction*, 11, 69–96.

Harvey, S. & Jarrett, K. (2013) A review of the game-centred approaches to teaching and coaching literature since 2006. *Physical Education and Sport Pedagogy*. DOI:10.1080/17408989.2012.754005

Hasbroucq, T. & Guiard, Y. (1991) Stimulus-response compatibility and the Simon effect: Toward a conceptual clarification. *Journal of Experimental Psychology*, 17, 246–266.

Hayes, N.A. & Broadbent, D.E. (1988) Two modes of learning for interactive tasks. *Cognition*, 28, 249–276.

Heilman, K. M., Nadeau, S. E. & Beversdorf, D. O. (2003) Creative innovation: Possible brain mechanisms. *Neurocase*, 9, 369–379.

Helsen, W.F., Starkes, J.L. & Hodges, N.J. (1998) Team sports and the theory of deliberate practice. *Journal of Sport and Exercise Psychology*, 20, 12–34.

Higgins, E.T. (1997) Beyond pleasure and pain. *American Psychologist*, 52, 1280–1300.

Higgins, E.T. (2000) Making a good decision: Value from fit. *American Psychologist*, 55, 1217–1230.

Higgins, E.T., Friedman, R.S., Harlow, R.E., Idson, L.C., Ayduk, O.N. & Taylor, A. (2001) Achievement orientations from subjective histories of success: Promotion pride versus prevention pride. *European Journal of Social Psychology*, 31, 3–23.

Hill-Haas, S.V., Coutts, A., Rowsell, G. & Dawson, B. (2008) Variability of acute physiological responses and performance profiles of youth soccer players in small-sided games. *Journal of Science and Medicine in Sport,* 11, 487–490.

Hill-Haas, S.V., Dawson, B.T., Coutts, A.J. & Rowsell, G.J. (2009) Physiological responses and time-motion characteristics of various small-sided soccer games in youth players. *Journal of Sports Sciences*, 27, 1–8.

Hill-Haas, S.V., Dawson, B.T., Impellizzeri, F.M. & Coutts, A.J. (2011) Physiology of small-sided games training in football: A systematic review. *Sports Medicine*, 41, 199–220.

Hirt, E.R., Levine, G.M., McDonald, H.E., Melton, R.J. & Martin, L.L. (1997) The role of mood in quantitative and qualitative aspects of performance: Single or multiple mechanisms? *Journal of Experimental Social Psychology*, 33, 602–629.

Hoffmann, J. (2009) ABC: A Psychological Theory of Anticipative Behavioral Control. In G. Pezzulo, M.V. Butz, O. Sigaud & G. Baldassarre (eds.), *Anticipatory Behaviour in Adaptive Learning Systems: From Psychological Theories to Artificial Cognitive Systems* (pp. 10–30). Heidelberg: Springer.

Hoffmann, J. (2010) Speculations on the origin of STM. *Psychologica Belgica*, 50, 175–191.

Hoffmann, J., Berner, M., Butz, M.V., Herbort, O., Kiesel, A., Kunde, W. & Lenhard, A. (2007) Explorations of Anticipatory Behavioral Control (ABC): A report from the Cognitive Psychology Unit of the University of Würzburg. *Cognitive Processing*, 8, 133–142.

Holt, N.L., Strean, W.B. & Bengoechea, E.G. (2002) Expanding the teaching games for understanding model: New avenues for future research and practice. *Journal of Teaching in Physical Education*, 21, 162–176.

Hommel, B., Müsseler, J., Aschersleben, G. & Prinz, W. (2002) The Theory of Event Coding (TEC): A framework for perception and action. *Behavioral and Brain Sciences*, 24, 849–878.

Hossner, E.J. (2001) Zehn Thesen zum Techniktraining. *Volleyballtraining*, 5, 66–71.

Hristovski, R., Davids, K. & Araújo, D. (2006) Affordance-controlled bifurcations of action patterns in martial arts. *Nonlinear Dynamics, Psychology, and Life Sciences*, 10, 409–444.

Hristovski, R., Davids, K. & Araujo, D. (2009) Information for regulating action in sport: Metastability and emergence of tactical solutions under ecological constraints. In D. Araujo, H. Ripoll & M. Raab (eds.), *Perspectives on Cognition and Action in Sport* (43–57). Hauppauge, NY: Nova Science Publishers, Inc.

Hristovski, R., Davids, K., Araujo, D. & Passos, P. (2011) Constraints-induced emergence of functional novelty in complex neurobiological systems: A basis for creativity in sport. *Nonlinear Dynamics-Psychology and Life Sciences*, 15, 175–206.

Huttenlocher, P.R. (1990) Morphometric study of human cerebral cortex development. *Neuropsychologia*, 28, 517–527.

Isen, A.M. (2000) Positive affect and decision making. In M. Lewis & J. Haviland-Jones (eds.), *Handbook of Emotions* (2nd Edition, pp. 417–435). New York: Guilford.

Isen, A.M., Daubman, K.A. & Nowicki, G.P. (1987) Positive affect facilitates creative problem solving. *Journal of Personality and Social Psychology*, 52, 1122–1131.

Jackson, R.C. & Farrow, D. (2005) Implicit perceptual training: How, when and why? *Human Movement Science*, 24, 308–325.

Jansen, D. (2006) *Von Organisationen und Märkten zur Wirtschaftssoziologie*. München/ Mering: Hampp.

Jeka, J.J., Kelso, J.A.S. & Kiemel, T. (1993) Spontaneous transitions and symmetry: Pattern dynamics in human four-limb coordination. *Human Movement Science*, 12, 627–651.

Jirsa, V.K. & Kelso, J.A.S. (2005) The Excitator as a Minimal Model for the Coordination Dynamics of Discrete and Rhythmic Movement Generation. *Journal of Motor Behavior*, 37, 35–51.

Johnson, J.G. & Raab, M. (2003) Take the first: Option-generation and resulting choices. *Organizational Behaviour and Human Decision Processes*, 91, 215–229.

Jones, C. & Farrow, D. (1999) The transfer of strategic knowledge: A test of the games classification curriculum model. *The Bulletin of Physical Education*, 25 (2), 103–124.

Kalinowski, A.G. (1985) The development of Olympic swimmers. In B.S. Bloom (ed.), *Developing Talent in Young People* (pp. 139–192). New York: Ballantine.

Kasof, J. (1997) Creativity and breadth of attention. *Creativity Research Journal*, 10, 303–315.

Keller, J. & Bless, H. (2006) Regulatory fit and cognitive performance: The interactive effect of chronic and situationally induces self-regulatory mechanisms on test performance. *European Journal of Social Psychology*, 36, 393–405.

Kelso, J.A. (1984) Phase transitions and critical behaviour in human bimanual coordination. *American Journal of Physiology-Regulatory, Integrative and Comparative Physiology*, 246, R1000–R1004.

Kelso, J.S. (1995) *Dynamic Patterns: The self-organization of brain and behaviour*. Cambridge: The MIT Press.

Kidman, L. and Lombardo, B.J. (2010) TGfU and Humanistic Coaching. In J.I. Butler and L.L. Griffin (eds.) *More Teaching Games for Understanding: Moving Globally* (pp. 171–186). Champaign, IL: Human Kinetics.

Kirk, D. & MacPhail, A. (2009) Teaching games for understanding and situated learning: Rethinking the Bunker-Thorpe model. In R. Bailey and D. Kirk (eds.), *The Routledge Physical Education Reader* (pp.269–283). Oxford: Routledge.

Kirton, M.J. (1976) Adaptors and innovators: A description and measure. *Journal of Applied Psychology*, 61, 622–629.

Krampen, G. (1996) *Kreativitätstest für Vorschul- und Schulkinder (KVS-P)* [Divergent thinking test for pre-school and school children]. Göttingen: Hogrefe.

Kuhl, J. (2000) A functional-design approach to motivation and self-regulation: The dynamics of personality systems interactions. In M. Boekaerts, P.R. Pintrich & M. Zeidner (eds.), *Handbook of Self-Regulation* (pp. 111–169). San Diego, CA: Academic Press.

Kunde, W., Koch, I. & Hoffman, J. (2004) Anticipated action effects affect the selection, initiation, and execution of actions. *Quarterly Journal of Experimental Psychology Section A*, 57 (1), 87–106.

Kurtzberg, T.R. & Amabile, T.M. (2000–2001) From Guilford to creative synergy: Opening the black box of team-level creativity. *Creativity Research Journal*, 13, 285–294.

Launder, A.G. (2001) *Play Practice: The games approach to teaching and coaching sports.* Champaign, IL: Human Kinetics.

Lee, T.D. (1988) Transfer-appropriate processing: A framework for conceptualizing practice effects in motor learning. In O.G. Meijer and K. Roth (eds.), *Complex Movement Behaviour: The motor-action controversy* (pp. 201–215). Amsterdam: North-Holland.

Lee, T.D. & Magill, R.A. (1983) The locus of contextual interference in motor-skill acquisition. *Journal of Experimental Psychology: Learning Memory, and Cognition*, 9, 730–746.

Lee, T.D., Magill, R.A. & Weeks, D.J. (1985) Influence of practice schedule on testing schema theory predictions in adults. *Journal of Motor Behaviour*, 17, 283–299.

Lieberman, M.D. (2000) Intuition: A social cognitive neuroscience approach. *Psychological Bulletin*, 126, 109–137.

Light, R. (2004) Coaches' experiences of games sense: Opportunities and challenges. *Physical Education & Sport Pedagogy*, 9, 115–131.

Lockwood, P., Jordan, C. & Kunda, Z. (2002) Motivation by positive or negative role models: Regulatory focus determines who will best inspire us. *Journal of Personality and Social Psychology*, 83, 854–864.

Loibl, J. (2001) *Basketball – Genetisches Lernen und Lehren: spielen – erfinden – erleben – verstehen.* Schorndorf: Hofmann.

Lumsden, K. (2001) *Complete Book of Drills for Winning Basketball.* Paramus, NJ: Prentice.

Mack, A. & Rock, I. (1998) *Inattentional Blindness.* Cambridge: MIT Press.

Maddox, W., Baldwin, G. & Markman, A. (2006) A test of the regulatory fit hypothesis in perceptual classification learning. *Memory and Cognition*, 34, 1377–1397.

Magill, R.A. (1998) Knowledge is more than we can talk about: Implicit learning in motor skill acquisition. *Research Quarterly for Exercise and Sport*, 69, 104–110.

Magill, R.A. & Hall, K.G. (1989) Implicit and explicit learning in a complex tracking task. Paper presented at the annual meeting of the Psychonomics Society, New Orleans, Louisiana.

Magill, R.A. & Hall, K.G. (1990) A review of the contextual interference effect in motor skill acquisition. *Human Movement Science*, 9, 241–289.

Martindale, C. (1981) *Cognition and Consciousness.* Homewood, IL: Dorsey.

Martindale, C. (1990) *The Clockwork Muse: The predictability of artistic styles*. New York: Basic Books.

Martindale, C. (1995). Creativity and connectionism. In S.M. Smith, T.B. Ward & R.A. Finke (eds.), *The Creative Cognition Approach* (pp. 249–268). Cambridge, MA: MIT Press.

Martindale, C. (1999) The biological basis of creativity. In R.J. Sternberg (ed.), *Handbook of Creativity* (pp. 137–152). Cambridge: Cambridge University Press.

Masters, R.S.W. (1992) Knowledge, knerves and know-how: The role of explicit versus implicit knowledge in the breakdown of a complex motor skill under pressure. *British Journal of Psychology*, 83, 343–358.

Masters, R.S.W. & Poolton, J.M. (2012) Advances in implicit motor learning. In A.M. Williams & N.J. Hodges (eds.), *Skill Acquisition in Sport: Research, theory and practice* (pp. 59–75). London: Routledge.

Mathisen, G.E. & Einarsen, S. (2004) A review of instruments assessing creative and innovative environments within organizations. *Creativity Research Journal*, 16, 119–140.

Maxwell, J.P., Masters, R.S.W., Kerr, E. & Weedon, E. (2001) The implicit benefit of learning without errors. *The Quarterly Journal of Experimental Psychology: Section A*, 54, 1049–1068.

McAloon, N.M. (1994) Connections (from the teacher's desk). *Journal of Reading*, 31, 698–699.

McNevin, N.H., Wulf, G. & Carlson, C. (2000) Effects of attentional focus, self-control, and dyad training effects on motor learning: Implications for physical rehabilitation. *Physical Therapy*, 80, 373–385.

McPherson, S.L. & French, K.E. (1991) Changes in cognitive strategies and motor skill in tennis. *Journal of Sport and Exercise Psychology*, 13 (1), 26–41.

Memmert, D. (2004) Ein Forschungsprogramm zur Validierung sportspielübergreifender Basistaktiken [A research programme for the validation of non-specific basic tactics]. *Sportwissenschaft [German Journal of Sport Science]*, 34, 341–354.

Memmert, D. (2006a) Developing creative thinking in a gifted sport enrichment program and the crucial role of attention processes. *High Ability Studies*, 17, 101–115.

Memmert, D. (2006b) Long-term effects of practical schedule on the learning and transfer of an applied motor skill. *Perceptual and Motor Skills*, 103, 912–916.

Memmert, D. (2006c) The effects of eye movements, age, and expertise on inattentional blindness. *Consciousness and Cognition*, 15, 620–627.

Memmert, D. (2006d) *Optimales Taktiktraining im Leistungsfußball [Optimal tactical training in professional soccer]*. Spitta-Verlag: Balingen.

Memmert, D. (2007) Can creativity be improved by an attention-broadening training program? An exploratory study focusing on team sports. *Creativity Research Journal*, 19, 1–12.

Memmert, D. (2009a) Noticing unexpected objects improves the creation of creative solutions: Inattentional blindness influences divergent thinking negatively. *Creativity Research Journal*, 21, 1–3.

Memmert, D. (2009b) Pay attention! A Review of Attentional Expertise in Sport. *International Review of Sport and Exercise Psychology*, 2, 119–138.

Memmert, D. (2010a) Testing of tactical performance in youth elite soccer. *Journal of Sports Science and Medicine*, 9, 199–205.

Memmert, D. (2010b). Creativity, expertise, and attention: Exploring their development and their relationships. *Journal of Sport Science*, 29, 93–104.

Memmert, D. (2010c) Development of creativity in the scope of the TGfU approach. In J.I. Butler & L.L.Griffin (eds.), *Teaching Games for Understanding: Theory, research and practice* (Second Edition) (p. 231–244). Champaign: Human Kinetics.

Memmert, D. (2011) Sports and Creativity. In M.A. Runco and S.R. Pritzker (eds.), *Encyclopedia of Creativity*, Second Edition, vol. 2, pp. 373–378. San Diego: Academic Press.

Memmert, D. (2013) Tactical creativity. In T. McGarry, P. O'Donoghue & J. Sampaio (eds.), *Routledge Handbook of Sports Performance Analysis* (pp. 297–308). Abingdon: Routledge.

Memmert, D., Baker, J. & Bertsch, C. (2010) Play and practice in the development of sport-specific creativity in team ball sports. *High Ability Studies*, 21, 3–18.

Memmert, D., Bischof, J., Endler, S., Grunz, A., Schmid, M., Schmidt, A. & Perl, J. (2011) World-level analysis in top level football. Analysis and simulation of football specific group tactics by means of adaptive neural networks. In C.L.P. Hui (ed.), *Artificial Neural Networks – Application* (pp. 3–12). ISBN: 789-953-307-188-6. Available from www.intechopen.com/articles/show/title/world-level-analysis-in-top-level-football-analysis-and-simulation-of-specific-football-group-tactic. (Accessed 2 December 2014).

Memmert, D. & Cañal-Bruland, R. (2009) The impact of approach and avoidance behaviour on visual selective attention. *Journal of General Psychology*, 136, 374–386.

Memmert, D. & Furley, P. (2007) "I Spy With My Little Eye!": Breadth of attention, inattentional blindness, and tactical decision making in team sports. *Journal of Sport and Exercise Psychology*, 29, 347–365.

Memmert, D. & Harvey, S. (2008) The Game Performance Assessment Instrument (GPAI): Some concerns and solutions for further development. *Journal of Teaching in Physical Education*, 27, 220–240.

Memmert, D., Hagemann, H., Althoetmar, R., Geppert, S. & Seiler, D. (2009) Conditions of practice in perceptual skill learning. *Research Quarterly for Exercise and Sport,* 80, 32–43.

Memmert, D. & Harvey, S. (2010) Identification of non-specific tactical problems in invasion games. *Physical Education and Sport Pedagogy*, 15, 287–305.

Memmert, D., Hüttermann, S. & Orliczek, J. (2013) Decide like Lionel Messi! The impact of regulatory focus on divergent thinking in sports. *Journal of Applied Social Psychology,* 43, 2163–2167.

Memmert, D. & König, S. (2007) Teaching games at elementary schools. *International Journal of Physical Education*, 44, 54–67.

Memmert, D. & Perl, J. (2005) Game intelligence analysis by means of a combination of variance analysis and neural networks. *International Journal of Computer Science in Sport*, 4, 29–38.

Memmert, D. & Perl, J. (2006) Analysis of game creativity development by means of continuously learning neural networks. In E. F. Moritz & S. Haake (eds.), *The Engineering of Sport 6,* Vol. 3 (pp. 261–266). New York: Springer.

Memmert, D. & Perl, J. (2009a) Game creativity analysis by means of neural networks. *Journal of Sport Science*, 27, 139–149.

Memmert, D. & Perl, J. (2009b) Analysis and simulation of creativity learning by means of artificial neural networks. *Human Movement Science*, 28, 263–282.

Memmert, D., Plessner, H. & Maßmann, C. (2009) Zur Erklärungskraft der "Regulatory Focus" Theorie im Sport. *Zeitschrift für Sportpsychologie*, 16, 80–90.

Memmert, D. & Roth, K. (2007) The effects of non-specific and specific concepts on tactical creativity in team ball sports. *Journal of Sport Science*, 25, 1423–1432.

Memmert, D., Simons, D. & Grimme, T. (2009) The relationship between visual attention and expertise in sports. *Psychology of Sport and Exercise*, 10, 146–151.

Memmert, D., Thumfart, M. & Uhing, M. (2014) *Optimales Taktiktraining im Leistungs-, Jugend- und Kinderfußball [Optimal tactical training in professional, youth and children soccer]*. Spitta-Verlag: Balingen.

Memmert, D., Unkelbach, C. & Ganns, S. (2010) The impact of regulatory fit on performance in an Inattentional Blindness paradigm. *The Journal of General Psychology*, 137, 129–139.

Mendelsohn, G.A. (1976) Associative and attentional processes in creative performance. *Journal of Personality*, 44, 341–369.

Mendelsohn, G.A. & Griswold, B.B. (1966) Assessed creative potential, vocabulary level, and sex as predictors of the use of incidental cues in verbal problem solving. *Journal of Personality and Social Psychology*, 4 (4), 423.

Mendelsohn, G. & Griswold, B. (1964) Differential use of of incidental stimuli in problem solving as a function of creativity. *Journal of Abnormal and Social Psychology*, 68, 431–436.

Menzel, R. (2001) Neuronale Plastizität, Lernen, Gedächtnis. In J. Dudel, R. Menzel & R. F. Schmidt (eds.), *Neurowissenschaft. Vom Molekül zur Kognition* (pp. 487–525). Berlin: Springer.

Metzler, M.W. (2000) *Instructional Models for Physical Education*. Boston: Allyn and Bacon.

Milgram, R.M. (1990) Creativity: An idea whose time has come and gone. In M.A. Runco & R.S. Albert (eds.), *Theory of Creativity* (pp. 215–233). Newbury Park: Sage.

Mitchell, S.A., Griffin, L. & Oslin, J.L. (1995) An analysis of two instructional approaches to teaching invasion games. *Research Quarterly for Exercise and Sport*, 66, A–65.

Mitchell, S.A. & Oslin, J.L. (1999) An investigation of tactical transfer in net games. *European Journal for Cognitive Psychology*, 4, 162–172.

Mitchell, S.A., Oslin, J.L. & Griffin, L.L. (2006) *Teaching Sport Concepts and Skills: A tactical games approach* (2nd ed.). Champaign: Human Kinetics.

Monsaas, J.A. (1985) Learning to be a world-class tennis player. In B.S. Bloom (ed.), *Developing Talent in Young People* (pp. 139–192). New York: Ballantine.

Most, S.B., Scholl, B.J., Clifford, E.R. & Simons, D.J. (2005) What you see is what you set: Sustained inattentional blindness and the capture of awareness. *Psychological Review*, 112, 217–242.

Moxley, S.E. (1979) Schema: The variability of practice hypothesis. *Journal of Motor Behaviour*, 11, 65–70.

Müsseler, I. (1995) *Wahrnehmung und Handlungsplanung*. Aachen: Shaker.

Nevett, M., Rovegno, I., Barbiaz, M. & McCaughtry, N. (2001) Changes in basic tactics and motor skills in an invasion-type game after a 12-lesson unit of instruction. *Journal of Teaching in Physical Education*, 20, 352–369.

Newell, D.G. (1986) Monoclonal antibodies directed against the flagella of Campylobacter jejuni: Cross-reacting and serotypic specificity and potential use in diagnosis. *J. Hyg*, 96, 377–384.

Nissen, M.J. & Bullemer, P. (1987) Attentional requirements of learning: Evidence from performance measures. *Cognitive Psychology*, 19, 1–32.

Olive, H. (1972) The relationship of divergent thinking to intelligence, social class, and achievement in high-school students. *The Journal of Genetic Psychology*, 121, 179–186.

Oslin, J. & Mitchell, S. (2006) Game-Centred Approaches to Teaching Physical Education. In D. Kirk, D. MacDonald & M. O'Sullivan (eds.), *The Handbook of Physical Education* (pp. 627–651). London: Sage.

Oslin, J.L., Mitchell, S.A. & Griffin, L.L. (1998) The Game Performance Assessment Instrument (GPAI): Development and preliminary validation. *Journal of Teaching in Physical Education*, 17, 231–243.

Ovens, A., Hopper, T. & Butler, J. (2012) Reframing curriculum, pedagogy and research. In A. Ovens, T. Hopper & J. Butler (eds.), *Complexity Thinking in Physical Education: Reframing Curriculum, Pedagogy and Research* (pp. 1–14). Routledge: London.

Passos, P., Araújo, D., Davids, K., Gouveia, L. & Serpa, S. (2006) Interpersonal dynamics in sport: The role of artificial neural networks and three-dimensional analysis. *Behaviour Research Methods*, 38, 683–691.

Partington, M., Cushion, C.J. & Harvey, S. (2014). An investigation of the effect of athletes' age on the coaching behaviours of professional top-level youth soccer coaches. *Journal of Sport Sciences*, 35, 403–414, *DOI:10.1080/02640414.2013.835063.*

Perl, J. (2004a) A neural network approach to movement pattern analysis. *Human Movement Science*, 23, 605–620.

Perl, J. (2004b) PerPot – a meta-model and software tool for analysis and optimisation of load-performance-interaction. *International Journal of Performance Analysis of Sport-e*, 4, 61–73.

Perl, J., Grunz, A. & Memmert, D. (2013) Tactics in soccer: An advanced approach. *International Journal of Computer Science in Sport*, 12, 33–44.

Perl, J., Memmert, D., Bischof, J. & Gerharz, C. (2006) On a first attempt at modelling creativity learning by means of artificial neural networks. *International Journal of Computer Science in Sport*, 5, 33–38.

Pinder, R.A., Davids, K.W., Renshaw, I. & Araújo, D. (2011) Representative learning design and functionality of research and practice in sport. *Journal of Sport and Exercise Psychology*, 33, 146–155.

Plessner, H., Unkelbach, C., Memmert, D., Baltes, A. & Kolb, A. (2009) Regulatory fit as a determinant of sport performance. *Psychology of Sport and Exercise*, 10, 108–115.

Port, R.F. & Van Gelder, T. (1998) *Mind as Motion: Explorations in the Dynamics of Cognition.* Cambridge, MA: The MIT Press.

Posner, M.I. (1980) Orienting of attention. *Quarterly Journal of Experimental Psychology*, 32, 3–25.

Prinz, W. & Hommel, B. (eds.) (2002) *Common Mechanisms in Perception and Action: Attention and performance XIX.* Oxford: Oxford University Press.

Prinz, W. (1990) A common-coding approach to perception and action. In O. Neumann & W. Prinz (eds.), *Relationships Between Perception and Action: Current approaches* (pp. 167–201). Berlin: Springer.

Prinz, W. (1997) Perception and action planning. *European Journal for Cognitive Psychology*, 9, 129–168.

Raab, M. (2003) Decision making in sports: Influence of complexity of implicit and explicit learning. *International Journal of Sport and Exercise Psychology*, 1, 310–337.

Rampinini, E., Impellizzeri, F.M., Castagna, C., Abt, G., Chamari, K., Sassi, A. & Marcora, S.M. (2007) Factors influencing physiological responses to small-sided soccer games. *Journal of Sports Sciences,* 25, 659–666.

Reber, A.S. (1967) Implicit learning of artificial grammars. *Journal of Verbal Learning and Verbal Behaviour*, 6, 855–863.

Reber, A.S. (1993) *Implicit Learning and Tacit Knowledge: An Essay on the Cognitive Unconscious*. Oxford: Oxford University Press.

Renzulli, J.S. (1994) *Schools for Talent Development: A practical plan for total school improvement*. Creative Learning Pr. Austin, TX: Prufrock Press.

Renzulli, J. & Reis, S.M. (2000) The schoolwide enrichment model: A focus on student productivity, strength and interests. In C.M. Callahan & H.L. Hertberg-Davis (eds.), *Fundamentals of Gifted Education Considering Multiple Perspectives* (pp. 199–211). New York: Routledge.

Richard, J-F., Godbout, P. & Gréhaigne, J.F. (2000) Students' precision and interobserver reliability of performance assessment in team sports. *Research Quarterly for Exercise and Sport*, 71, 85–91.

Richard, J-F., Godbout, P., Tousignant, M. & Gréhaigne, J.F. (1999) The try-out of team sport performance assessment procedure in elementary school and junior high school physical education classes. *Journal of Teaching in Physical Education*, 18, 336–356.

Rink, J.E., French, K.E. & Graham, K.C. (1996) Implications for practice and research. *Journal of Teaching in Physical Education*, 5, 490–502.

Rossi, T., Fry, J.M., McNeill, M. and Tan, C.W.K. (2007) The Games Concept Approach (GCA) as a mandated practice: Views of Singaporean teachers. *Sport, Education and Society*, 12, 93–111.

Roth, K. (2005) Taktiktraining [Training of Tactics]. In A. Hohmann, M. Kolb & K. Roth (eds.), Handbuch Sportspiel [Handbook of Sport Games] (pp. 342–349). Schorndorf: Hofmann.

Roth, K. & Kröger, C. (2011) *Ballschule – Ein ABC für Spielanfänger* [Ball School – An introduction to game play]. Schorndorf: Hofmann.

Roth, K., Kröger, C. & Memmert, D. (2002) *Ballschule Rückschlagspiele [Ball school racket sports]*. Schorndorf: Hofmann.

Roth, K., Memmert, D. & Schubert, R. (2006) *Ballschule Wurfspiele [Ball school invasion games with the hand]*. Schorndorf: Hofmann.

Runco, M.A. (2007) *Creativity – Theories and Themes: Research, Development, and Practice*. Burlington: Elsevier Academic Press.

Runco, M.A. & Sakamoto, S.O. (1999) Experimental Studies of Creativity. In R.J. Sternberg (ed.), *Handbook of Creativity* (pp. 62–92). Cambridge: Cambridge University Press.

Runco, M.A. & Albert, R.S. (1986) The threshold theory regarding creativity and intelligence: An empirical test with gifted and nongifted children. *Creative Child and Adult Quarterly*, 11, 212–218.

Ryan, R.M. & Deci, E.L. (2000) Self-determination theory and the facilitation of intrinsic motivation, social development, and well-being. *American Psychologist*, 55, 68–78.

Safrit, M.J. & Wood, T.M. (1989) *Measurement Concepts in Physical Education and Exercise Science*. Champaign: Human Kinetics.

Sauseng, P., Klimesch, W., Doppelmayr, M., Pecherstorfer, T., Freunberger, R. & Hanslmayr, S. (2005) EEG alpha synchronization and functional coupling during top-down processing in a working memory task. *Human Brain Mapping*, 26, 148–155.

Savelsbergh, G.J.P., Kamper, W., Rabius, J., De Koning, J. & Schöllhorn, W. (2010) New methods to learn to start in speed skating: A differential learning approach. *International Journal of Sport Psychology*, 41, 415–427.

Schmidt, R.A. (1975) A schema theory of discrete motor skill learning. *Psycholoical Review*, 82, 225–260.

Schmidt, R.A. (2003) Motor schema theory after 27 years: Reflections and implications for a new theory. *Research Quarterly for Exercise and Sport,* 74 (4), 366–375.

Schmidt, R.A. & Wrisberg, C.A. (2004) *Motor Learning and Performance.* Champaign, IL: Human Kinetics.

Schöllhorn, W.I., Hegen, P. & Davids, K. (2012) The nonlinear nature of learning – A differential learning approach, *The Open Sport Science Journal,* 5, 100–112.

Schöllhorn, W.I., Michelbrink, M., Beckmann, H., Trockel, M., Sechelmann, M. & Davids, K. (2006) Does noise provide a basis for the unification of motor learning theories? *International Journal of Sport Psychology,* 37, 34–42.

Schöllhorn, W., Michelbrink, M., Welminski, D. & Davids, D. (2009) Increasing stochastic perturbations enhance skill acquisition and learning of complex sport movements. In D. Araujo, H. Ripoll & M. Raab (eds.), *Perspectives on Cognition and Action in Sport* (pp. 59–73). Hauppauge, NY, United States: Nova Science.

Schöner, G., Haken, H. & Kelso, J.A.S. (1986) A stochastic theory of phase transitions in human hand movement. *Biological Cybernetics,* 53, 247–257.

Scott, G., Leritz, L. E. & Mumford, M. D. (2004) The effectiveness of creativity training: A quantitative review. *Creativity Research Journal,* 16, 361–388.

Shah, J., Higgins, E.T. & Friedman, R.S. (1998) Performance incentives and means: How regulatory focus influences goal attainment. *Journal of Personality and Social Psychology,* 74, 285–293.

Shea, C.H. & Kohl, R.M. (1991) Composition of practice: Influence of the retention of motor skills. *Research Quarterly for Exercise and Sport,* 62, 187–195.

Shea, C.H., Kohl, R. & Indermill, C. (1990) Contextual interference: Contributions of practice. *Acta Psychologica,* 73, 145–157.

Shea, C.H. & Morgan, R.B. (1979) Contextual interference effects on the acquisition, retention, and transfer of a motor skill. *Journal of Experimental Psychology: Human Learning and Memory,* 5, 179–187.

Shea, C.H. & Wulf, G. (2005) Schema theory: A critical appraisal and reevaluation. *Journal of Motor Behaviour,* 37, 85–101.

Shea, C.H. & Zimny, S.T. (1983) Context effects in memory and learning movement information. In R.A. Magill (ed.), *Memory and Control of Action* (pp. 1454–1466). Amsterdam: North Holland.

Sherwood, D.E. (1996) The benefits of random variable practice for spatial accuracy and error defection in a rapid aiming task. *Research Quarterly for Exercise and Sport,* 67, 35–43.

Sherwood, D.E. & Lee, T.D. (2003) Schema theory: Critical review and implications for the role of cognition in a new theory of motor learning. *Research Quarterly for Exercise and Sport,* 74, 376–382.

Simons, D.J. & Chabris, C.F. (1999) Gorillas in our midst: Sustained inattentional blindness for dynamic events. *Perception,* 28, 1059–1074.

Simonton, D.K. (1988) *Scientific Genius: A psychology of science.* Cambridge: Cambridge University Press.

Simonton, D.K. (1996) Creative expertise: A life-span development perspective. In K.A. Ericsson (ed.), *The Road to Expert Performance: Empirical evidence from the arts and sciences, sports, and games* (pp. 227–253). Mahwah, NJ: Erlbaum.

Simonton, D.K. (1999) Talent and its development: An emergenic and epigenetic model. *Psychological Review,* 106, 435–457.

Simonton, D.K. (2003) Scientific creativity as constrained stochastic behaviour: The integration of product, person and process. *Psychological Bulletin,* 129, 475–494.

Smith, S.M., Ward, T.B. & Finke, R.A. (eds.) (1995) *The Creative Cognition Approach.* Cambridge: MIT Press.

Speelman, C.P. & Kirsner, K. (1997) The specificity of skill acquisition and transfer. *Australian Journal of Psychology*, 49 (2), 91–100.

Starkes, J.L. & Allard, F. (1993) *Cognitive Issues in Motor Expertise.* Amsterdam: Elsevier Science Publishing.

Sternberg, R.J. (1985) *Beyond IQ.* New York: Cambridge University Press.

Sternberg, R.J. (1988) A three-faceted model of creativity. In R.J. Sternberg (ed.), *The Nature of Creativity* (pp. 124–147). New York: Cambridge University Press.

Sternberg, R.J. (ed.) (1999) *Handbook of Creativity.* Cambridge: Cambridge University Press.

Sternberg, R.J. & Lubart, T.I. (1991) An investment theory of creativity and its development. *Human Development*, 34, 1–31.

Sternberg, R.J. & Lubart, T.I. (1992) Buy low and sell high: An investment approach to creativity. *Current Directions in Psychological Science*, 1, 1–5.

Sternberg, R.J. & Lubart, T.I. (1995) *Defying the Crowd.* New York: Free Press.

Sternberg, R.J. & Lubart, T.I. (1999) The concept of creativity: Prospects and paradigms. In R.J. Sternberg (ed.), *Handbook of Creativity* (pp. 3–15). Cambridge: Cambridge University Press.

Straka, G.A. (ed.) (2000) *Conceptions of Self-Directed Learning.* New York: Waxmann.

Strayer, D.L., Drews, F.A. & Johnston, W.A. (2003) Cell phone induced failures of visual attention during simulated driving. *Journal of Experimental Psychology: Applied*, 9, 23–32.

Summerville, A. & Roese, N.J. (2008) Self-report measures of individual differences in regulatory focus: A cautionary note. *Journal of Research in Personality*, 42, 247–254.

Tallir, I.B., Lenoir, M., Valcke, M. & Musch, E. (2007) Do alternative instructional approaches result in different game performance learning outcomes? Authentic assessment in varying game conditions. *International Journal of Sport Psychology*, 38, 263–282.

Thurstone, L.L. (1938) *Primary Mental Abilities. Psychometric monographs.* Chicago: Chicago University Press.

Toh, K. & Woolnough, B. (1994) Science process skills: Are they generalisable? *Research in Science and Technological Education*, 12, 31–42.

Torrance, E.P. (1988) The nature of creativity as manifest in its testing. *The Nature of Creativity*, 43–75.

Tucker, G.R. (1996) Some thoughts concerning innovative language education programmes. *Journal of Multilingual and Multicultural Development*, 17, 315–320.

Tuckman, B. W. & Hinkle, J. S. (1986) An experimental study of the physical and psychological effects of aerobic exercise on schoolchildren. *Health Psychology: Official Journal of the Division of Health Psychology, American Psychological Association*, 5 (3), 197.

Turner, A.P. (1996) Teaching for understanding: Myth or reality? *Journal of Physical Education, Recreation and Dance*, 67, 46–48.

Turner, A.P. & Martinek, T.J. (1992) A comparative analysis of two models for teaching games. *International Journal of Physical Education*, 29, 15–31.

Vallerand, R.J. (2001) A hierarchical model of intrinsic and extrinsic motivation in sport and exercise. In D.G. Roberts (ed.), *Advances in Motivation in Sport and Exercise* (pp. 212–235). Champaign: Human Kinetics.

Von Stein, A. & Sarnthein, J. (2000) Different frequencies for different scales of cortical integration: From local gamma to long range alpha/theta synchronization. *International Journal of Psychophysiology*, 38, 301–313.

Walinga, J. (2007) *The Power of Focus: Unlocking creative insight and overcoming performance barriers.* Doctoral dissertation. Retrieved from http://hdl.handle.net/1828/224 (Accessed 2 December 2014).

Ward, T.B., Finke, R.A. & Smith, S.M. (2002) Creativity and the Mind – Discovering the Genius Within. Cambridge: Perseus Publishing.

Watt, D. (2000) The centrencephalon and thalamocortical integration: Neglected contributions of periaqueductal gray. *Consciousness and Emotion*, 1, 91–114.

Weeks, D.L. & Kordus, R.N. (1998) Relative frequency of knowledge of performance and motor skill learning. *Research Quarterly for Exercise and Sport*, 69, 224–230.

Werth, L., Denzler, M. & Förster, J. (2002) Was motiviert wen? Worauf der Fokus liegt, entscheidet über den Erfolg. *Wirtschaftspsychologie*, 2, 5–12.

Werth, L. & Förster, J. (2007a) How regulatory focus influences consumer behaviour. *European Journal of Social Psychology*, 37, 33–51.

Werth, L. & Förster, J. (2007b) Regulatorischer Fokus. Ein Überblick. *Zeitschrift für Sozialpsychologie*, 38, 33–42.

Williams, A.M., Davids, K. & Williams, J.G. (1999) *Visual Perception and Action in Sport*. London: E & FN Spon.

Wright, C., Atkins, S., Jones, B. & Todd, J. (2013) The role of performance analysts within the coaching process: Performance Analysts Survey "The role of performance analysts in elite football club settings." *International Journal of Performance Analysis in Sport*, 13, 240–261.

Wrisberg, C.A. (1991) A field test of the effect of contextual variety during skill acquisition. *Journal of Teaching in Physical Education*, 11, 21–30.

Wrisberg, C.A. & Lui, Z. (1991) The effect of contextual variety on the practice, retention, and transfer of an applied motor skill. *Research Quarterly for Exercise and Sport*, 62, 406–412.

Wulf, G. (1991) The effect of type of practice on motor learning in children. *Applied Cognitive Psychology*, 5, 124–135.

Wulf, G. & Schmidt R.A. (1994) Feedback-induced variability and the learning of generalized motor programs. *Journal of Motor Behaviour*, 26, 348–361.

Wulf, G. & Toole, T. (1999) Physical assistance devices in complex motor skill learning: Benefits of a self-controlled practice schedule. *Research Quarterly for Exercise and Sport*, 70, 265–272.

Yamamoto, K. (1965) Effects of restriction of range and test unreliability on correlation between measures of intelligence and creative thinking. *British Journal of Educational Psychology*, 35, 300–305.

Young, D.E., Cohen, M.J. & Husak, W.S. (1993) Contextual interference and motor skill acquisition: On the processes that influence retention. *Human Movement Science*, 12, 577–600.

Zanone, P.G. & Kelso, J.A.S. (1992) Evolution of behavioural attractors with learning: Nonequilibrium phase transitions. *Journal Experimental of Psychology: Human Perception and Performance*, 18, 403–421.

Glossary

1-Dimension games as a principle of fostering tactical creativity means basic-element games with one tactical aim and multiple repetitions of similar situations.

Breadth of attention is the term used to refer to the number and range of stimuli that a subject attends to at any time.

Context-Interference effects refer to the advantage of random conditions for motor and perceptual learning, which can be explained by permanent cognitive reconstruction process that increase retention stability. In contrast to blocked conditions, in which the same action plan can always be used, the tasks are constantly changed in random conditions so that the action plan has to be reconstructed.

Deliberate coaching as a principle of fostering tactical creativity means that trainers and teachers shall give no instructions before and during game play that narrow the focus of attention of the acting players.

Deliberate motivation as a principle of fostering tactical creativity means that trainers and teachers shall give promotion instructions before game play to enlarge the generation of extraordinary solutions.

Deliberate play as a principle of fostering tactical creativity means using uninstructed game forms in play-oriented and at-first-sight unstructured activities in the absence of coaching and feedback.

Deliberate practice as a principle of fostering tactical creativity means task-centred practice in more advanced games to repeat and explore seldom but adequate solutions. It is based on careful instructions and detailed and immediate feedback.

Differential learning means that alternating and fluctuating are meaningful components of the motor learning process and these factors have to be explicitly supported in training programmes (e.g. mistakes are important). The central point is that the biggest steps in the learning process are achieved when the organism has to always newly adapt to given situations.

Diversification as a principle of fostering tactical creativity means to use different motor skills in basic-element games.

Explicit learning relates to appropriation processes within intentional and target-oriented learning activities, which means the person "knows" that they are educated (in contrast to implicit learning).

Game analysis software allows the study of individual tactical behaviour of the players (e.g. feints in one-on-one-situations), the tactical interactions of a group of players (e.g. specific combinations in the offensive), and the general game strategy of a team (e.g. playing more defensively).

Game test situations are simple game forms with clearly defined game ideas and fixed numbers of players as well as defined rules and environmental conditions. The fundamental idea is basic constellations with clearly allocated roles in order to create recurring and consistent conditions with many repetitions for the participants. In order to analyse the creative actions, a video of the recorded behaviour is subsequently rated with regard to specific concepts by several independent experts.

Group tactics are tactical tasks which have to be solved through the cooperation of several team members or position groups. Such position groups are, for instance, strikers or midfielders, but also players in certain areas (e.g. left and right wing) or players from different positions, that move across those areas in a particular moment.

Identification of gaps is a basic tactical task which includes the tactical requirement to make spatial decisions by using gaps effectively. The players should recognise the optimal gap, or if no gaps become available the ball must be passed within the team.

Implicit learning is an inductive process, by which help knowledge is gained in such a way that neither the process of knowledge acquisition nor the gained knowledge is available to conscious awareness.

Inattentional blindness is the failure to detect an unexpected object if attention is diverted to another task. When attention is assigned to a different object, an unexpected object is often not perceived, even though it is located in the field of vision.

Investment approach to creativity by Sternberg and Lubart (1991) integrated different theoretical creativity models into one framework. This framework includes the Componential Theory by Amabile (1983), the Systems Approach by Csikszentmihalyi (1988), the Synectic Model by Gordon (1961) and the "Triarchic Theory of Intelligence" by Sternberg himself (1985). Furthermore, it includes results from studies on personality (Barron, 1965), problem solving (Getzels and Csikszentmihalyi, 1976), creative styles (Kirton, 1976), and different environmental influences (Simonton, 1988).

Neural networks are a type of computer algorithm which consists of a grid or matrix of neurons. The dimension of this neuron matrix determines the dimension of the network. Neurons are trained with data and so build clusters of similar input data, without needing any additional information. These clusters define types of input data and thereby help to recognise and identify test data after the training phase. A given test input is recognised by the network as corresponding to the cluster to which it is most similar, and is therefore identified by the type (e.g. name, specification) of that cluster.

Nonlinear dynamical systems theory emphasises biological movement systems under the constraints of their natural environments and the importance of qualitative changes in the system, rather than dealing merely with quantitative ones. It defines control parameters as informational variables that can guide a system between different organisation states. Order parameters are defined as collective variables that describe the organisation of such systems.

Regulatory focus theory proposes two modes of self-regulation: a focus on accomplishments and aspirations is labeled as a **promotion focus** to regulate pleasure, while a focus on safety and responsibilities is called a **prevention focus** to avoid suffering.

Support and orienting is a basic tactical task which includes the tactical requirement to take an optimal position on the playing field at the right time. The player should learn the adequate seeking out of positions in the spaces that are easy to pass to.

Tactical creativity approach integrated six empirically supported principles and recommendations (**D**eliberate Play, 1-**D**imension-Games, **D**iversification, **D**eliberate Coaching, **D**eliberate Motivation, **D**eliberate Practice) for fostering tactical creativity in team and racket sports. It is based on the Investment Approach to Creativity by Sternberg and Lubart (1991) and entails the basic components of attention, motivation, environment, and expertise.

Tactical creativity or divergent tactical thinking ability is defined at the behavioural level as the unusualness, innovativeness, statistical rareness or even uniqueness of solutions to a related sport situation in team and racket sports.

Tactical intelligence, convergent tactical thinking ability or game sense refers at the behavioural level to the ability to find the ideal solution to a given problem in a specific situation in team ball sports.

Tactical transfer means that tactical knowledge and understanding can transfer from the performance of one game to the performance of another game.

Taking the ball near the goal is a basic tactical task which includes the tactical requirement to transport the ball, together with team mates, to a finishing space. The player should learn to pass the ball in a certain direction in relation to the target area and bridge a distance as large as possible.

Teaching games for understanding approach by Bunker and Thorpe (1982) focuses initially on teaching an understanding of the tactical dimensions of game play (i.e. what to do), before the teacher/instructor focuses on the development of the students' technical skills associated with the game (i.e. how to do). The primary aim is to place the player in problem solving situations, where game sense, game playing ability, or even game performance may be developed.

Team and racket sports such as football, basketball, team handball, field hockey, volleyball and racket sports including, tennis, table tennis and badminton.

Variability of practice hypothesis suggests that a wide range of parameter variability (e.g. movement velocity, muscle force, limb angles) introduced through variable training will be more effective for parameter motor learning in complex motor skills than constant, more drilled practice.

Index

The following index has been developed with consideration of key terms listed in the glossary. Each major concept is listed with sub-concepts indented with page numbers.